ALL ABOUT HARRY

Congo entrepreneur, RAF Fl/Lt., Haganah agent,

Israeli Air Force Colonel, diplomat and businessman

A BIOGRAPHY BY: DR. ALAN SWARC

London

Published by New Generation Publishing in 2019

Copyright © Dr. Alan Swarc 2019

First Edition

The author asserts the moral right under the Copyright, Designs and Patents Act 1988 to be identified as the author of this work.

All Rights reserved. No part of this publication may be reproduced, stored in a retrieval system or transmitted, in any form or by any means without the prior consent of the author, nor be otherwise circulated in any form of binding or cover other than that which it is published and without a similar condition being imposed on the subsequent purchaser.

ISBN
        Paperback: 978-1-78955-774-9
        Hardback: 978-1-78955-775-6

www.newgeneration-publishing.com

New Generation Publishing

Acknowledgements

There are many people, associated in one way or another with Harry, who have contributed their thoughts and time in helping me to complete this book.

Most prominent and selfless in her research was my cousin Annette from Petach Tikvah.
She not only provided photographs and documents but was also particularly energetic in arranging very productive contacts with family members of Harry who lived as far afield as the USA (Hedy, a niece), Israel (Mariana, a great-great niece), Belgium (Ben, his son and his mother, Rosette, and also Claire and Georges Vandecasteele, a niece and nephew) Ben, himself, was instrumental in introducing me to « Mac » Max Felix, who maintained a close relationship with Harry. My thanks to him also for giving of his time.

Annette also arranged interviews for me with Israeli contemporaries of Harry who were former senior officers in the fledgling IAF (Sherut Ha'Avir). These officers were gracious enough to meet me in their homes and share their memories. My thanks therefore go to Dan Tolkowski , Yehoshua Gilutz and Alex Zieloni for their invaluable contributions to this story

In view of my limited knowledge of Hebrew I am grateful to those who gave of their time in the laborious work of translating articles, letters and official documents. Thanks also go to my son Joel whose computer savvy and regard to the aesthetic quality of the photographs and captions reproduced in this book ensured they were of a high standard. Un grand Merci! to my cousin Maurice who supplied useful information on Harry's period in the IAF and an amusing anecdote. Also, most importantly, my gratitude to my wife Dot who played a great part in proofing the final manuscript.

I would also like to recognise the assistance of the Israeli Journalist Shlomo Nakdimon and Lt. Colonel (reserves.) Eli Eyal who had both written newspaper articles about Harry's adventures. They delved into their personal archives to freely provide me with their own work.

Archive material on Harry's war time service with the Polish Air Force was graciously provided by the Polish Institute and Sikorski Museum, London. Despite the fact that it was virtually all in Polish, I was able to make some use of the extensive documentation. I am indebted for the effort put in by the Institute's staff to meet my request for information.

I could not end without giving a special mention of my conversations with Harry's wife, Lilian and their offspring, Micky and Mina They received me with great warmth and interest in my project. For what must have been, sometimes, painful memories, they recounted their relationships with Harry until his death in November 1989.

Although much of what I have written is derived from family and friends' anecdotes and documents, I have also incorporated some of my own research at the National Archives at Kew (abbreviation: N.A). I remain sincerely grateful for the helpful guidance given by its staff.

Any mistakes or misconceptions in the text are fully my own and I apologise for any unintended offence I may have caused by their unfortunate inclusion.

CONTENTS

Preface 1
Introduction 2
Chapter 1: The formative years 1906-1928 5
Chapter 2: The first Belgian Congo venture 1928 -1939 .. 8
Chapter 3: The War Years 1939- 1945 19
Chapter 4: The Glorious Years 1945-51 32
Chapter 5: The second Belgian Congo venture 1951-1959 58
Chapter 6 Congolese politics before and after independence 1959-1961 70
Chapter 7 Harry's third family 1961-1971 95
Chapter 8: The Fight for Justice 1971-1989 107
Chapter 9: Family Views 133
Chapter 10 Conclusion 139
Appendix1: Tursz-Fredkens Family Tree 141

LIST OF PLATES

1. (a) Rosette, Harry's first wife; (b) Harry aged 31 18
2. (a) Harry in RAF uniform; (b) Letter to his commanding officer 30
3. (a) Yehuda Arazi; (b) Harry's own Manuscript (Excerpt) 31
4. (a) Ida in Paris during war. 50
5. Ida and Annette in Haifa; (b) Harry and Ida in Tel Aviv 51
6. Harry, Ralla, Georges and Doris in Courtrai [2 photos]........52
7. Harry, Ida and Annette in Kutu [2 photos]............................53
8. Harry and Ida in Paris 54
9. RAF Certificates of Competency: [2 photos].........................55
10. Harry's forged Canadian passport: [2 photos]......................56
11. David Ben Gurion at "Shechounot Ha'Katzenim" [2 photos] 57
12. The Vandecasteele family in the Congo................................65
13. (a) Harry's house in Kutu; (b) Ida in Leopoldville...............66
14. (a) A boat called *"Ida";* (b) Harry and Ben in Kutu [3 photos] 67
15. Work at the sawmill in Kutu [2 photos] 68
16. Ida and Harry prior to departure from Congo......................69
17. Letter Harry wrote to Kasabubu 77
18. Kasavubu, Lumumba, and King Baudouin in Leopoldville 91
19. Presentation of Israeli delegation to President Kasavubu [2 photos]...92
20. Lumumba, Mpolo and Okito 93
21. Harry as economic advisor to President Kasavubu 94
22. (a) Ben's wedding; (b) Harry and Ben in Brussels.............104
23. (a) Annette's Wedding in Tel Aviv; (b) Harry and Schmulik 105
24. (a) David Ben Gurion at reception in Tel Aviv; (b) Harry and Pinhas Sapir..106

25. (a) Reunion of Cairo Haganah Cell in Tel Aviv (b) Harry and Avrahami 128

26. (a) Harry's IAF service record; (b) Letter from Aharon Remez 129

27. Dan Tolkowski [2 photos]. 130

28. (a) Annette, Lilian and Harry; (b) Annette with Harry and his children 131

29. Harry with Eli Eyal 132

"Every even-handed biography of a complete life has to deal with private matters and to present its subject as fully as possible, even if the subject, when alive, might have preferred to keep these matters obscured – or at least not open to the world."

Vikram Seth (Author of "Two lives", 2005)

Preface

To attempt to write a biography of a man who only fleetingly appears in the history of the State of Israel and who, by consequence, may not even be considered among its lesser heroes, is an act of faith. Faith that somehow out of the recollections of those few who still recalled his passage and, more prosaically, out of some archival research, would emerge an accurate picture of a man whose life was far from mundane.

In relating the exploits of *"Freddy"* Fredkens, David Ben Gurion, in his diary of the War of Independence, quietly revealed the existence of a Haganah agent, whose real surname was Tursz-Fredkens. Other equally brief references to Fredkens appeared in a book on the Arab/Israeli conflict of 1948/49 (*"Oh, Jerusalem"* by Collins and Lapierre) and in the chronicles of the Israeli Air Force. However, other than for some Israeli newspaper articles, there was little other public record of his activities.

So why embark, some 17 years after his death and with so little basic information, on the time-consuming task of researching and writing his biography? The answer lies in the enthusiasm of his various families (he was married three times) to join with me in bringing to light, warts and all, the various facets of the life of *"Harry"*.

Now, thirteen long years later, the job is finally done.

Introduction

He regarded himself as one of the unsung heroes of Israel. Yet he would not attempt to class himself on the same scale as the legendary military or diplomatic heroes of Israel, who were his contemporaries in the early days of the State. He felt nevertheless, that he had carried out many sensitive missions abroad, in his own quiet and selfless way, which had been all too easily forgotten. In the last years of his life, when financial difficulties and health problems increasingly affected his quality of life and that of his young family, he felt betrayed by the lack of support coming from an establishment that, in his own eyes, was virtually turning its back on him.

How did this all come about to a man who at the height of his powers, had been an RAF pilot, a colonel in the Israeli air force, an entrepreneur, a diplomat and on first-name terms with many in the ruling hierarchy of Israeli politics?

His full name, Henryk Grzegorz Tursz-Fredkens was, even by Israeli standards, difficult to accommodate and so, except in official documents, he was variously known as *"Harry"* or *"Freddy"* Fredkens. Consequently, throughout this book, we will refer to him as Harry.

This then is the story of his life. It is not a eulogy but a portrait of a complex man whose life took extraordinary turns, sometimes as a result of an unexpected event or a chance encounter.

Unlike many of his contemporaries, he did not come from a Zionist background, was not at home in the Hebrew language and culturally was more an Englishman than an Israeli. Yet he was swept up in the 1940s by the Zionist fervour which gripped many Jews abroad and found himself at the centre of adventures which were the stuff of *"boys' own"* comics. He was carefree and paid little attention to the potentially dangerous consequences of his actions. He could not be excused on the grounds of youth because many of his exploits were carried out in his early forties, when wiser counsels ought normally to have prevailed. He was, in short, a one-off and the reader should take this into account when judging a man who, despite his evident flaws and failings, always embraced life to the full and gave much of himself to those family and friends who were nearest and dearest to him.

As an enthusiastic and skilled pilot from an early age, no distance was too great for Harry, nor any destination too risky. He moved from Europe to Africa to the Far East, solely based on the range of the type of plane he was flying at the time and whether it was a civilian aircraft or one of the many he grew accustomed to in the RAF.

He spent different periods of his life in Poland, Belgium, Great Britain, the Belgian Congo and Israel and was fluent in many languages including English, French, Flemish and Lingala (Congo dialect) but, strangely, not Hebrew. He personally knew David Ben Gurion and many other personalities within the ruling establishment in the early years of the State of Israel. He was entrusted with many delicate missions before and after its creation, some of which were at the risk of his life. Yet he carried them out with a dash and élan that earned him, at the time, the respect of many of his contemporaries. Later he would complain that memories were short.

His business ventures often ended in financial failure, but his few successes encouraged the adventurer in him to continue to strike out for gold. Towards the end of his life his lack of financial acumen nearly spelled ruin for him and his young family. Finally, a military pension acquired with great difficulty and a fair amount of lobbying by his friends and family, enabled him to finish his years in comparative dignity.

There were many distinct periods in his life, and, in this book, they have been treated as separate episodes as they spanned different locations and often different marital circumstances. Harry always yearned for variety, adventure and wealth and it is in the pursuit of this quest that he met many challenges or arrived at crossroads, where an instantaneous decision would decide his fate for years to come. He was particularly adept at taking on different personae as the needs of the moment dictated. All the while he was a gifted raconteur with a wonderful sense of humour and a taste for the good things of life, be they attractive women, classy cars or simply good food. Many from within his various families have described him as being larger than life, where legend and reality were sometimes indistinguishable from one another.

To write the biography of such a man, where one yearns for the objective truth, is a daunting task but not to attempt it would have been a disservice to all those who admired and loved him and felt that he was deserving of a recognition that was not fully accorded to him in his lifetime.

In researching the material for this biography, besides noting the personal elements which lie at its core, account has also been taken of contemporary events which furnished the backdrop to each stage of Harry's life. Therefore, short historical references to the war-time RAF, the Belgian Congo and the British Mandate in Palestine have been added where this helps to inform the reader. The personal reminiscences of family, friends and colleagues are often quoted and where possible corroborated from other sources by the author. Part of one chapter refers to Harry's own account of one of his great adventures during his war time service in the RAF. The original source is a long unpublished manuscript, which relates his involvement in spiriting away, out of Egypt, a legendary Haganah (Pre-State Jewish military forces) officer wanted by the British Mandate police.

Chapter 1: The formative years 1906-1928

[This chapter briefly explores Harry's family background, early development and sense of adventure]

The reconstruction of Harry's early years with his family was difficult to determine, as there was little by way of written record and those who were his contemporaries during his formative years had long passed on. I was, nevertheless, able to glean from his nieces, nephews and great-niece facts and impressions which were passed on to them by their own parents during their lifetime. The overwhelming memory is that of a man who, despite his faults, was very much admired and loved. His outstanding characteristic was that he made people laugh, none more so than his beloved mother. In January 1986, just after his 80th birthday party in Netanya, Harry wrote to his youngest sister Evelyn in the USA: *"When I am alone at home, I often talk with our unforgettable Mummy and she is waiting for me to join her"*.

By this time Harry was physically impaired. He had only about 40 % vision and could not go out for walks unaccompanied.

Harry's parents, Moschek and Sonia had left Russian-controlled Warsaw with Harry in July 1907. Possibly the major incentive was the series of pogroms which followed the first Russian Revolution of 1905. This convinced many Jews to seek not only safety but economic well- being in either Western Europe or the United States. Within a few years the dynasty created by Harry's grandparents, Aron and Mikla Tursz, comprising ten children, was spread across Europe. In the case of Moschek, now aged 29, Antwerp, as the centre of the Jewish diamond trade, offered the prospect of a welcome into an existing Jewish community and an outlet for his skills. He and his family were joined in Antwerp by Moschek's youngest brother, Sigismund.

Four years after Harry's birth, Sonia gave birth to a daughter, Mary and in 1914 to a second daughter, Ralla. Within months the First World War broke out with an attack on Belgium. Moschek, who had foreseen such an eventuality, gathered up his family and took a boat to England before the Germans broke through Antwerp's defences. They were welcomed in England by Moschek's younger brother, Konrad, and his family who had emigrated some years earlier. Harry who was now 8 years old was enrolled in a primary school, where he struggled to improve his English. In 1917 he acquired a third sister with the birth of Evelyn. Initially at the Barnsbury Church of England School, Harry then went on to the fee-paying Merchant Taylor's School for his secondary education. There, he adopted the attributes and style of an English gentleman. He was tall and lanky, good at sports and, though cursed with a strange accent, his knowledge of the English language was of a very high standard. Altogether he was a very satisfactory student.

In 1920, when war time restrictions on travel were lifted, Moshek took his wife and daughters back to Antwerp. Harry was left as a boarder in England to complete his secondary education but in 1923 he briefly re-joined his parents.

Given his technical aptitudes, it was decided that Harry would study mechanical engineering at Ghent University. He had not lost his knowledge of French and Flemish and the transition was therefore comparatively easy for him. His parents being of modest means, he had to support himself throughout his university days by taking on a series of different jobs. It was during this period that he made the acquaintance of several students from Palestine and they introduced him to the Zionist society, of which he soon became the secretary. Harry was now a Zionist supporter and, later, this was to dictate the course of his future. An opportunity presented itself for him to learn flying and this he took up with great enthusiasm. He qualified as the best pilot on his course. Thereafter, he was never happier than when he was personally at the controls of an aircraft, either civilian or military.

When the time came to leave university in 1928, Harry had two job offers. Either to work as a mining engineer in China or to become engaged in palm oil exploitation in the Belgian Congo. Both jobs required flying skills. He tossed a coin and the Congo won out. His contract was to last for three years.

Chapter 2: The first Belgian Congo venture 1928 -1939

[If nothing else, this chapter provides insights into Harry's volatile and impulsive character, his cavalier attitude to his family's needs and his amoral nature]

In 1928 at the age of twenty-two Harry was eager to make his mark. The Congo, still then under Belgian rule, offered immense opportunities to a young man of his ambition and intelligence. Ruled by Belgium since 1886, it had been the personal fiefdom of Leopold II, who established there a very centralised authority under a Governor General in Leopoldville, present-day Kinshasa. Here the colonial authorities ensured that there were European–reserved areas to ensure racial segregation from the Africans. The effective authority in the Congo was a trinity of the Catholic Church, an extensive civil service and military force and business interests. Catholic missionaries were engaged in primary and vocational educational work and they also improved medical services. A Concordat with the Vatican, signed by Belgium in 1906, recognised the primacy of the Church in these areas. Whilst the everyday tasks of administration were performed by a massive corps of colonial civil servants, law and order was strenuously enforced by the Belgian-officered *"Force Publique."* The third element, big business, ensured that the Congo was regarded almost exclusively as a field for European investment, which precluded any significant role for Africans. Europeans directly controlled the local labour force, supplied it with health care and food and ensured its productivity. By the end of the 1920s, mining, especially of copper and diamonds, was the mainstay of the economy, having far outdistanced agriculture.

Harry's first job allowed him to appreciate these various facets of life in the Congo. He was certainly not disturbed by the lack of rights of the natives living under one of the more reactionary colonial regimes in Africa. Indeed, he learnt to emulate the lifestyle of the Belgian expatriates he came across and developed a love for the country. He adjusted well to the tropical climate despite its all year-round heat and humidity but appreciated the rainy season in October. He worked on the Kuilu River for a Unilever company, the *Huileries du Congo Belge*, exploiting palm oil. During this time, he learnt to speak Lingala, the local dialect but, as his contract was not renewed, he returned to Antwerp in 1931.

He soon found temporary work with the Braunschweig *Café du Congo* company and involved himself in one of the local Zionist groups. There he met Rosette Hilfman and began a courtship. Rosette who was born in Suriname, Dutch Guyana, was the daughter of Pinkus Hilfman and Grace Bueno de Mesquida whose family were Sephardi Jews. According to Rosette she did not seriously contemplate marriage with Harry at the time. However, he was very tall and slim, always immaculately dressed and so intelligent that soon, the *"silly girl of twenty-two"* as she described herself, was swept off her feet by his attentions. She later learnt that Harry had made a bet with his friends that she would marry him. Influenced by his persuasive manner, she agreed to go with him to the Congo once he had established a livelihood for them there. There was then a separation for over a year. During that period Rosette had to pretend to her parents that she was receiving regular letters from the Congo, which was not usually the case.

In the Congo Harry had launched himself into the lumber business. Based in the town of Kutu at the junction of Lake Leopold II and the Fimi river, he set up a sawmill to which were floated trees cut down on the other side of the lake at Ebabaka. There Harry had been granted an exclusive concession by the Belgian authorities. The enterprise was run under the name of *Compagnie Africaine d'Entreprises Commerciales (CADEC)*. Most of his employees were from the Kundu tribe. At the sawmill, power for the steam engine came from wood–burning furnaces. Second quality wood was used to assemble packing cases for use by breweries (this was before the advent of cardboard), whilst the best wood was selected for export. The produce of the sawmill was then transported on flat barges, pushed by one of the boats that Harry had designed and built, to Leopoldville on the Congo River. Harry had personally designed the house at Kutu, which was built, together with the sawmill, on a promontory into the lake. The house was shaped like an immense native hut and contained several rooms. A large balcony surrounded the house from which Harry could see the sawmill nearby. From there two opposing staircases led down a few steps to the ground. A few hundred metres away were the sheds which constituted the sawmill. After cutting through the massive tree trunks, the planks were graded and laid out outside in the open air. Although he employed a foreman, Harry was forever personally supervising the work both at the sawmill and in the forests. Whenever new tools were required, Harry used his engineering skills to improvise the equipment on the spot. A story goes that he even fashioned a set of metallic false teeth for one of his workers. In addition to the saw-mill staff, Harry also employed *"boys"* in his house as servants. One of the longest serving house servants was Jules who was responsible for the kitchen

Harry soon found his niche among other expatriates in the colonial society. His affable nature and quick sense of humour endeared him to his neighbours who, nevertheless were often an air flight away. He had a great reputation as a pilot and flew a white bi-plane over the great swathes of forests to pinpoint the best areas for his tree-cutting gangs.

He was referred to by the natives as *"Katende"*, (Lingala for *"White Eagle"*). An old village chief, the King of the Dekese tribe, Ikengo Samo, once told Ben, Harry's son, and his friend *"Mac"*, who were visiting him in the early 1980's, that, before the war, he and Harry had to kill a number of natives who were rebelling against his authority. The king remembered meeting Harry for the first time when he emerged exhausted from the forest on one of his reconnaissance missions. After a few beers they got to know each other and shared a few jokes. Before he left, Harry asked him, to his puzzlement, to clear a large stretch of forest for him, ready for his next trip.

Some weeks later, there was a strange noise in the sky as Harry flew overhead. He managed to land in the cleared area prepared for him by the King's warriors. When the King asked him where he had come from, he pointed upwards. Ikengo Samo then asked him if he had met any dead missionaries up above. The missionaries he had met always told him that when they died, they went to heaven. Harry quickly gave him his own critical views on missionaries with whom he shared a mutual dislike. After telling this story, the King brought out a large metal trunk, which he opened in front of them. It had been left with him for safekeeping by Harry before he left the Congo in 1959. Inside were Harry's hunting rifles and various items of clothing. They would be waiting for him if he ever returned.

An extraordinary story that Harry had told many years later in Brussels, which *"Mac"* thought, at the time, was exaggerated, was actually confirmed to him and Ben by the King. The story goes that when Harry set off for war in October 1940, leaving his past life behind him, he made his way by river from Leopoldville to Port Francqi on the Kasai river. Here the railway line towards Kenya began. This was close to the village of the King and Harry visited him and told him of his plans to join the British army in Nairobi. The next day Harry waited on the railway platform among a large crowd for his train. Suddenly he noticed the arrival of the King accompanied by hundreds of warriors carrying spears, bows and arrows. The crowd, taken aback by this war party, parted to allow a passageway. When the King reached Harry, he told him in all seriousness that they were going off to war with him. Although highly honoured by the King's gesture, it took all of Harry's diplomatic and persuasive powers to explain that this was just not feasible in the present circumstances. Nevertheless, he promised to pass on to the British military authorities the King's desire to join the war against the Italians. Satisfied with this assurance the King led his men back to their village. On 2 November Harry was formally recruited into the British army in Nairobi and the King's offer was not taken up .He did not see Harry again for many years.

Let us now go back a few years.

In September 1932 Harry had finally made a return visit to Antwerp and he and Rosette were married two months later in a Jewish wedding ceremony. They left for the Congo via Portugal, their ship first arriving in Lobito in Angola and then Leopoldville. In Kutu Rosette found to her horror that the house had no electricity and little furniture. During the first days they had to sleep on planks. Harry had grown too used to living with the minimum of facilities. He had made little provision for his new wife who was used to a comfortable existence in the bourgeois surroundings of Antwerp. But with the gradual improvement in their quality of life, she soon grew to love the Congo as much as he did. In October 1934, whilst Harry was away on one of his flights, she gave birth at the Leopoldville hospital run by the nuns. And so, Mark Bernard later to be always known as Ben came into the world.

That year the world trade recession also hit the Congo and Harry had to find alternative sources of income. These included the illegal hunting of elephants for the ivory trade and trading in coffee and copal. It was during this period that Harry would disappear for weeks on end, flying off on some *"business venture"* or other. He never left her much money *"just a bag of coins"* according to Rosette. Harry throughout his life always had a hankering for travel and would often leave his home at a moment's notice. Each of his former wives viewed his long absences as being one of his most annoying habits. But he never failed to bring back some expensive gifts to make up for this. When I interviewed Rosette at her flat in Brussels in December 2006 (She was 97 then), she also mentioned Harry's other annoying habit of continually making complicated business calculations on scraps of paper, which he promised would bring in *"millions"* but, in practice, never did. He could never understand her lack of intellectual curiosity in his far-fetched ideas. But then she knew how quickly Harry moved from one project to another when he became disenchanted with the existing one. Harry was gifted in many ways, but patience and perseverance were not his major attributes.

In May 1936, at Rosette's insistence, they returned to Antwerp with the baby. This gave them the opportunity to show off Ben to both sets of grandparents and other members of the family. After a year or so they returned to the Congo. This was to be the last time that Harry saw his parents.

Harry was often in financial difficulties. Once arriving by boat in Leopoldville, he was accosted by Antoine Delporte, the head of the Belgian Congo" *Sureté* "and a squad of police. After a brief discussion, Harry came over to Rosette and said that he had to go with them to sort out a problem at the bank. She later found out that there was a question of some unpaid cheques. In the meantime, not wishing to leave Rosette by herself, Delporte escorted her to the hotel. Harry reappeared a little later having sorted out his *"bank problem"*. But far graver in Rosette's eyes, than his financial ineptitude, was Harry's infidelity. Like many European expatriates he had developed a taste for local women. She found out that at the hotel he had regularly stayed with one of two women. Finally, in 1939, these continual affairs led to a breakup of their marriage and Rosette sued for divorce. To Harry's chagrin, not only did he lose contact with his son, now aged 5 but Rosette subsequently married Antoine Delporte. This was the policeman, who had briefly detained Harry. Harry would tell his acquaintances that he intended to retrieve his son, but this proved to be wishful thinking.

A year after the war in Europe had broken out Harry, in a fit of patriotism for the land of his schooldays, enlisted in the British army. He would have done so earlier but for the fact that the authorities in the Belgian Congo remained wary of joining the war effort. The Belgian Government-in-Exile located in London since the invasion and defeat of Belgium in May 1940 were reluctant to commit their forces in the Congo to hostile activity against the Italians in East Africa. In September 1940 these forces comprised 300 white officers and NCOs and 13,000 native troops. The British War Office's major concern was that the copper belt on the North Rhodesian border, which was adjacent to Katanga in the Belgian Congo, was vulnerable to attack from Axis forces (Italy had declared war on France and Great Britain on 10 June 1940) and therefore, sought to increase its military presence in the area. Furthermore, the mineral wealth of the Congo was of immediate interest to the British and would become, because of the availability of uranium, equally so for the Americans. The Belgian authorities, for their part, were concerned that German elements in neutral Portuguese Angola might attempt an attack northward towards Leopoldville and its strategic assets. For these reasons the establishment of a British military Mission in Leopoldville and Stanleyville seemed desirable to both the British and the Belgians. Initially the British felt it best to retain the local troops in the Congo, to maintain stability and deal with any fifth column activities. However, the Belgian officer corps itself became restless towards October 1940. It therefore supported the *"Ligue d'Action Patriotique"* in its demands on the Belgian authorities in London to release forces for use outside the Congo. On 3 August the Italians had begun the occupation of British Somaliland to the east of Kenya. In view of impending military action by the British, Harry decided the time had come for him to join the fray. It was in these circumstances that Harry, as a Pole and not as a Belgian subject went to the British Military Mission and offered his services. He was told to make his way to Kenya and report for duty in Nairobi. At the end of October 1940 Harry suddenly ceased his business activities leaving his creditors, his personal representative, his former wife and the native labour without sufficient financial resources. After he left the house at Kutu in the safekeeping of his cook, Jules, he promised to return once the war was over. He made the same promise to his son Ben who, by then, was attending the Dames du Sacree Coeur primary school in Leopoldville.

Shortly after his departure his company, *"CADEC"*, was dissolved by its creditors and on 11 December 1940 Harry was personally declared bankrupt. Fortunately for him, the subsequent sale of the Company's assets by auction was enough to pay off the creditors and leave a fair sum to be credited to his personal bank account. However, because of Harry's constant failures to keep up with maintenance payments to Ben, Rosette had to go to court in May 1944 to attach the account. This court action by Rosette was somehow picked up by the financial division of the Air Ministry. At the time Harry was a pilot in the Polish Air Force in the UK and was claiming an allowance in respect of Ben's upkeep. The Air Ministry demanded to be satisfied that Harry was indeed using the allowance for its intended purpose.[1] This early example of Harry's cavalier attitude to his finances was to be repeated many times in the future and was ultimately to lead to severe financial problems.

Now briefly turning our attention from Central Africa to the war in Europe, we pause to review the situation of Harry's sisters and parents in Antwerp. They, to say the least, were not reassured when both Belgium and Holland declared neutrality in the event of a future conflict which might arise between England and France on the one hand and Germany on the other. The first to translate her anxiety into action was Harry's eldest sister Mary. She speedily made her way with her two daughters first to Palestine and then in 1940 to Mexico, where her husband, Nathan, awaited her. Harry's second sister Ralla continued living with her husband, Alfons Vandecasteele and her two children in Coutrai, where she was to remain for the entire war. The youngest sister, Evelyn, was married to Walter Mandel, but as an Austrian citizen he was taken to an internment camp as an undesirable alien immediately the Germans invaded Belgium. Fortunately, before they reached Antwerp on 18 May 1940, Evelyn had left with her three-month old twin daughters for neutral Portugal. As she left, her mother Sonia placed her wedding ring in her hand. It was almost a sign that they would never meet again. In Lisbon, Evelyn was later joined by her husband who had managed to bribe his way out of the internment camp. They then left for the USA, which they reached in November 1940. Hedy Sonia, the latest addition to the family, later reflected how generous Harry could be. When she was 18 years old, he sent her a very large cheque because he wanted her to go to finishing school in Switzerland. Hedy, however had other ideas and spent the

---

[1] Letter to General H.Q. of the Polish Air Force. 21.3.45

money to pay for her wedding. Harry was not at all happy but clearly later forgave her.

With their children gone, Moschek and Sonia Tursz were now virtually alone. This was compounded by the fact that having disapproved of Ralla's pregnancy and subsequent marriage to a Catholic in 1933, their relationship with her remained strained. Was this then a case of children abandoning their parents or of parents insisting that while they could not themselves face leaving Antwerp, they actively encouraged their daughters, in the absence of their husbands, to flee to safety with their young children? I suspect, the latter. In the late 1930s some 80% of Antwerp's Jews were engaged in the diamond trade, but by 1940 many had taken the opportunity to flee to Cuba, England, Palestine, Portugal or the USA taking as many precious stones as they could. Most Jewish diamond cutters and merchants, who did not flee, were deported and murdered by the Nazis in the camps in 1942.

Rosette, Harry's first wife,
at 97 years old. (Photo taken in her flat in Brussels in 2006)

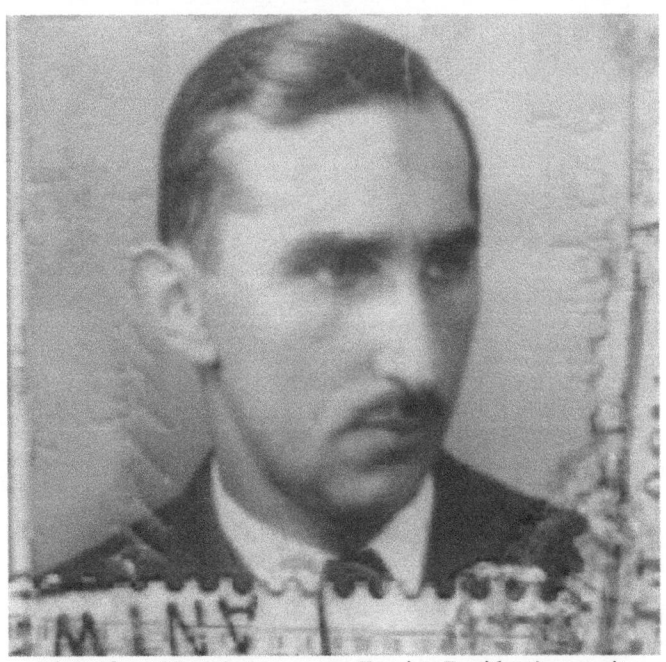

Photo from Harry's temporary Foreign Resident's permit.
Antwerp, 13 November 1936

Chapter 3: The War Years 1939- 1945

[Free from the bonds of marriage and professional responsibilities, Harry set off into a new adventure. This chapter explores the development of his army and, subsequently, RAF career]

Harry's skills in mechanical engineering were put to good use in the East Africa Army Service Corps (E.A.A.S.C.) based in Nairobi. However, there is no indication that he was involved in combat operations in the actual Campaign. This eventually resulted in the Italians complete defeat. Nevertheless, Harry could content himself that his service in the *"No.9 Heavy Repair Shop"*, maintaining Army lorries, was described as exemplary by his commanding officer. He was commended for:

"his sound knowledge of mechanical engineering and being an able and practical mechanic"

On 27 February 1942, after the successful end of the East Africa Campaign, Harry suddenly found himself discharged from the British Army, with the temporary rank of sergeant and the *"Star of Africa"* campaign medal. He had served with the colours one year and 118 days. He was then immediately transferred to the Cairo area and to the Polish Army under British Command. This came as something of an unwelcome surprise for him, as he had only a smattering of Polish and could not even write in the language. Nevertheless, as a Polish citizen. he was not given any choice. He soon found himself in Palestine with a posting to the First Polish Independent Carpathian Rifle Brigade. In view of his previous army experience he was assigned to the Infantry Officer Cadets School where, much to his dislike, he was to spend a year in Polish uniform.

During this period, the fate of Jews in German Occupied Europe took a turn for the worse. After the Wannse Conference of January 1942, when a plan for their physical extermination was finally approved, Gestapo forces prepared to round up the existing local Jewish communities and transport them to camps in the East. In France, Belgium and Holland, this measure was to be carried out with the assistance of local police forces, to give it the appearance of legitimacy and avoid undue alarm. In Belgium the process started in July 1942 with individual Jews receiving notices to report for compulsory labour. When this subterfuge didn't work, roundups took place. The Jews were taken to former military barracks at Malines (Mechelen in Flemish). From the beginning of August two *"transports"* a week, of a thousand Jews each, left the barracks for an *"unknown"* destination in the East. Harry's parents were arrested by the Belgian Fascist Militia in Antwerp on 12 August 1942 and were transported to Auschwitz, but Harry was not to know of their fate until much later. Out of a total Jewish population of 39,000 living in Belgium in 1939, 62% were murdered in Auschwitz. Amongst those who remained and survived in Belgium, was Ralla and her 3 children, the last of whom, Claire, was born in Courtrai in 1943. It was because of her pregnancy that Ralla was exempted from the compulsory labour call-up. This was the second time that she had avoided a round-up of Jews. The first time was when the Germans came to arrest the British owner of the shop where she was working. Keeping her cool, she spoke to the SS officer in German and he, assuming that she was Christian, ceased interrogating her and departed. Since the deportation of her husband, Alfons, to a labour camp, Ralla had been living hidden in a room above the shop. She avoided wearing the compulsory yellow star in the street.

Meanwhile, during Harry's stint in the Polish army there was a significant reorganisation instigated by the Polish Prime Minister and Commander in Chief, General Sikorski, then resident in London. To meet his desire to create an armoured division, a parachute brigade and a Polish air force in the UK, he needed to transfer Polish troops from the Middle East. However, the lack of allied shipping delayed the transport of 8,000 of them for nearly a year. Finally some 4,300 arrived in Liverpool in February 1943. Amongst them was Harry. Because of his previous flying experience (he had already flown 1,860 hours in various civilian aircraft), he was now destined for the Polish Air Force under British command.[2]. He formally enlisted on 21 March 1943 and on his application form he described himself as a Roman Catholic. Perhaps not surprising given Polish attitude to Jews in that era.

A month later, with the rank of flight sergeant, he was sent on several training courses to prepare him for flying duties. After a year he was posted to his first active squadron. For the next ten months he did various stints in a few squadrons all involved in aircraft target-towing activities. These provided gunnery practice for AA batteries on land and at sea. These were not duties that Harry particularly enjoyed as they required a fair amount of night flying which, given adverse weather conditions, were particularly stressful. Nevertheless, Harry persevered and was promoted in 1944 first to Pilot Officer and six months later to Fl/ Lt.

One of the documents which emerged from Harry's war time service was a letter he wrote to his Polish

---

[2] My contacts with the Polish Institute and Sikorski Museum in Princes Gate, London, produced from their archives, pages of documentation in Polish on Harry's war time service. The only documents in English were copies of Harry's occasional correspondence with his superior officers. Usually requests for postings to other units. One example is included at the end of this chapter

commanding officer in July 1944 in which he pleaded for the opportunity to increase his night-time flying hours in order to qualify for a specialised training course. He also requested exemption from the regulation which limited participation in the course to officers under 35 years of age. At the time Harry was over 38. In the letter, however, he only admitted to 37 as he had, on his application form to the RAF, deliberately or otherwise, given his year of birth as 1906. Closing the letter, he apologised for being still unable to write *"in our own language"* . Harry's stylish use of language reflected how much Harry had benefited from an English education in his early years. A report on his character by his Polish commanding officer in October 1944, mentioned his tendency to exaggerate his past.

But was it all really an exaggeration? Read on:

A narrative of Harry's war time experiences from 1944 to 1946 is encapsulated in a lengthy manuscript he wrote in 1976. Here Harry takes centre stage as he describes his part in the rescue of Yehuda Arazi, *"The Scarlet Pimpernel of the Haganah"* as Harry described him. Written with the intent of publication, the original manuscript entitled *"Wanted: Yehuda Arazi",* remained unpublished and dormant for many years after Harry's death. It was retrieved by his widow, Lilian, in December 2006 from the attic of her bungalow in Israel. The manuscript was written in an engaging style with a great emphasis on verbatim conversations which were reputed to have taken place between the main players, Harry being the most prominent.

Every detail of how Harry secretly flew Yehuda Arazi out of Cairo in May 1945 to Bari in Italy is told with great relish. He also reveals details of his own life, which are corroborated in other parts of this book. However, Harry, inexplicably, leaves out of the manuscript specific events, such as his divorce and his second marriage, even though these are no less pertinent to his personal history than his frequent references to his son. Again, some of Harry's recollection of actual historical events, which are meant to enhance the narrative, are not always chronologically correct. One must conclude that Harry's intention, being the great raconteur that he was, was to write a *"spiffing yarn"* which, although based on real events, reflected a fair amount of poetic licence.

In January 1945 he was posted to the RAF Ferry Unit in Cairo. According to him he had requested an overseas posting in order to temporarily distance himself from his girlfriend, *"Pat"*[3] in England. His new role was to convey surplus war planes to overseas RAF airfields in Europe, Africa and Asia.

Once in Cairo he frequented one of two Jewish servicemen's clubs where members of Palestinian forces in the British army would gather.

At first, his appearance in RAF rather than Palestinian forces uniform led to some suspicion, but as he related his connection to his Zionist activities in pre-war Belgium,

---

[3] His romance with « *Pat* » seems to have been a somewhat tempestuous affair. Harry claimed that once in Cairo he realised that this was not an infatuation, but that he was really in love with her. Four weeks after his arrival he heard from « *Pat* » that she had got a transfer to the Scottish Hôspital in Cairo. Hearing this news, he immediately went to the adjutant's office and filled out an application for permission to marry, but it was not to be. Shortly after, Harry received a telegram from her parents to announce the sad news that « *Pat* » had been involved in a fatal car accident in London..
Proof of this fateful relationship came in the form of a photo of « *Pat* » in Annette's possession. On the back was written in her hand: «*To Harry, from one mortal being to another* ».

he made friends very quickly. It wasn't too long before he was approached by Hagana members, Shalom Levin (*"Asaf"*) and Levi Avrahami with a request to convey sums of money to their contacts in Bari, Italy. It was explained that this was to assist illegal immigration to Palestine from the Mediterranean ports. Despite the risks involved (the real the possibility of a court-martial), Harry agreed to pick up the money from "*Vaad Haspel*" (Labour Federation offices) on one of his occasional visits to Tel Aviv. He would then carry out a mission whenever a trip to Bari presented itself.

After a number of these trips, without discovery, Harry was approached to carry out a much more spectacular mission. This involved smuggling on board a fugitive from the CID in Palestine and flying him to Bari. The man was Yehuda Arazi, a senior Haganah officer who had carried out various operations against the Colonial power. In 1933 Yehuda Arazi had been an officer in the Palestine British Police, but in1936 he resigned and left for Poland to procure arms for the Haganah. From 1943 onwards he was wanted by the British CID for having stolen 5000 rifles and had to go into hiding. As the net closed in, the Haganah seized the opportunity to move him to Cairo.

Despite the complex logistics involved, Harry accepted this new mission with alacrity and set about formulating a plan with the Haganah cell.

Eventually Arazi was covertly brought by train from Rehovot in Palestine to Alexandria in a British army uniform and hidden in Levi Avrahami's flat. In his manuscript, Harry describes Arazi as being:

"Of medium build, very pale with silver grey hair, between 34 and 36 years old. He walked with a slight limp and spoke with a pronounced Polish accent"

Before Harry was given the final go-ahead, a team of senior Haganah officials from Palestine arrived to check out his bona fides and his plan. Basically, Arazi was to be given the name and credentials of an existing officer in the polish section of the RAF who was on leave in England. A suitable uniform would be provided, and Harry would steal blank RAF documentation from his base which would then be falsified with a photo of Arazi, his new Polish name and other identifying data. In view of Arazi's accent it was essential that he appeared to be the genuine article. Equally, to avoid standing out, it was necessary for Arazi to gain a suntan like other RAF personnel in Cairo. Harry vouched for the discretion of the crew on the Wellington bomber that would be used on the, so-called, rescue mission.

From Harry's Manuscript it is clear, during their brief time together, that he developed a strong bond with Arazi. Under the spell of the latter's persuasive powers and charm he promised to come to Palestine and join the Haganah once he was demobilized from the RAF.

It was agreed that the mission was to be set in motion for the end of May 1945.

This duly took place and involved getting Arazi in his Polish uniform on to the airbase and training him how to get into the Wellington bomber without arousing the suspicion of the RAF Police.

The details of the flight plan, involving a stop at various locations before the last leg to Bari, were very complex but, nevertheless, were accomplished successfully. They eventually landed in Bari on 5 June. In Bari Arazi then contacted Haganah operatives and bid farewell to Harry. As a final gesture, he gave Harry his Polish Air Force cap badge as a souvenir.[4]

Arazi's activities in Italy hit the headlines in April 1946 when he attempted to smuggle about 1000 Jewish refugees

---

[4] Many years later, well after Arazi's untimely death in 1959, Harry presented the badge to his widow together with a copy of his manuscript.

out of the port of La Spezia for a clandestine journey to Palestine. In a confrontation with the British occupying power he mounted a public relations exercise which finally succeeded in allowing the ship, *"La Fede"*, to sail away in a blare of adverse publicity for the British.

As previously pointed out, there were many surprising omissions from Harry's manuscript. Harry's initial contacts with Palestinian Jews in the RAF, who were to be among his close acquaintances in later life would have been worthy of comment and yet were not mentioned at all. For instance, there was the young Fl/Lt. Dan Tolkowski . Dan, at the time, was the RAF Movements Officer at Lydda Airport (Now Ben Gurion Airport). Harry was asked by his Haganah friends in Cairo to introduce himself to Dan, who could be a useful contact for him in the future. Much later in 1953, Dan became the commander of the Israeli Air Force. There was also Squadron Leader Yehoshua Gilutz, responsible for ground maintenance on RAF aircraft. Then, in his 90th year, Yehoshua told me that Harry would often recount graphic tales of life in the Congo and his hunting exploits. At the time Yehoshua unjustly, as it turns out, viewed all these tales with a certain amount of skepticism. Finally there was Fl/Lt. Alex Zieloni, also a mechanical engineer who, after a stint as Chief of Staff of Sherut Ha'Avir became commander of the Tel Nof air base in August 1948 .All these Palestinians had been studying either mechanical or aeronautical engineering in England in the late1930's and had volunteered for the RAF when war broke out. As with Harry, they all subsequently saw service in the IAF (Israeli Air Force) and this shared experience cemented a bond of comradeship which proved helpful to Harry in later years.

Certainly, the most glaring omission in the manuscript is any mention of Harry's divorce from Rosette and his subsequent marriage in January 1946. Admittedly, this came some time after Yehuda Arazi was safely delivered to Italy and therefore had no bearing whatsoever on the tale. Nevertheless, they were significant milestones in Harry's life.

The events surrounding Arazi were recalled in two letters which Harry received in the 1970's. The first was from Teddy Kollek, then mayor of Jerusalem:

"Dear Freddy,
I was truly amazed-and happily surprised-to receive your letter. It has been years, but of course I remember.
I did in fact accompany Eliyahu Golomb [Then head of the Haganah] *to Cairo when he visited Levi Avrahami to look you over.*
With all good wishes for success with your book and kind personal regards.

Yours,
Teddy"

The second letter was from Levy Avrahami the former police chief of Jerusalem. This is an extract:

Jerusalem, February 14, 1972
"Yehuda Arazi was smuggled into Egypt by Israel Lavy wearing British Army uniform with false papers on a train from Rehovot to Alexandria at the beginning of May 1945.
Eliyahu Golomb came to Cairo in the middle of May 1945. At the end of the same month you took Yehuda on your famous flight to Italy.
Eliyahu Golomb died on June 11,1945.

Yours,
Levi"

These two letters underline Harry's risky collaboration, whilst still in the Royal Air Force, with forces that were fiercely opposed to British rule in Mandate Palestine.

In September 1946, after a brief trip to Belgium, Harry flew to the Congo .But he was not alone. During a stop-over in Tel Aviv he fulfilled his promise and picked up his new wife and her daughter. He hadn't seen them since his return to England in April to get demobilized. They joined him in his single-engine light aircraft for a long flight to the Congo. Unfortunately, however, the Proctor crash-landed near Luxor in Egypt with engine trouble and the three of them had to continue by scheduled flight.

Harry's initial acquaintance with Ida Szwarc-Birnbach and her daughter Annette had come about during one of his frequent visits to his cousins in Tel Aviv. In this house, Ida and Annette lived in a couple of rooms on the ground floor. They had arrived from France in August 1945 after any hope of the return from Auschwitz of Ida's husband, Judah Szwarc (my uncle), had long been abandoned.

Ida's parents, the Birnbachs, were emigrating from Frankfurt to Palestine. In 1936, whilst they were in transit in Paris, Ida met Judah, originally from Poland. Later, with the consent of her parents (She was only eighteen years old), she returned from Palestine and they married in August 1937. Annette was born in May 1939 on the same day that her parents' French naturalization papers came through.

Judah was arrested during the second round-up of Jews in Paris in August 1941 and was deported to Auschwitz in March 1942. Ida and Annette remained hidden with Judah's mother. Thanks to Ida's ingenuity and sang-froid they all managed to survive until the liberation of Paris in August 1944. In the meantime, like all other Jews, she was obliged to wear the Star of David on her clothing under pain of arrest and deportation.

A year later Annette was declared an orphan, and this enabled Ida to acquire from the British an entry certificate for her into Palestine. As a registered welfare assistant, Ida accompanied her and hundreds of Jewish orphans from Europe who were shipped out to Palestine by the Jewish Agency. A photograph taken at the time shows Ida and Annette, both smartly dressed and wearing sunglasses, coming off the boat in Haifa as if at the end of a summer holiday cruise. It was always a cardinal rule of Ida's that, whatever the circumstances, she would not appear in public unless she was made up and suitably dressed for the occasion. Annette, to this day, applies the same rule.

Initially, mother and daughter were sent to a temporary camp at Athlit, run by the Agency. After a short period, they were able to leave for Tel Aviv where Ida had her family. Nevertheless, those early days in a strange land were difficult for both but they managed to live in relative comfort. By all accounts, after they were introduced, Ida and Harry were immediately attracted to each other. Despite their thirteen-year difference in age, he successfully courted her. Annette was entranced by this giant of a man in RAF uniform who loved children. After a religious marriage in Tel Aviv on 24 January 1946, Harry had to return to his duties in Cairo with a promise that he would return to them.

Fl/ Lt Harry Fredkens as a pilot in a Polish Squadron of the RAF

Harry's letter to his Polish commanding officer, 1944

Yehuda Arazi (Haganah Officer)

```
                        WANTED : YEHUDA ARAZI.
CHAPTER I.
        It is seventeen years since Yehuda Arazi left u
the evening of my life, it is still like a breath of
remember the one who was a great and loyal friend.

        When I returned to Tel-Aviv from a trip abroad,
 me at the airport informed me of Yehuda's death, a w
 a year's long losing and hopeless fight against a li
unforgiving illness.

        The next morning I went to the cemetry to visi
I stood, quite alone and lost in thought beside his
place, I wondered how many people really knew the de
to Yehuda "The scarlet Pimpernel of the Haganah".-

        I recalled our first meeting in Cairo and the
crossing and recrossing of our paths, which had led
lasting friendship. I could still see his whimsical
twinkle in his steely grey eyes as at the end of eac
he would say, " Till next time Freddy".
```

Excerpt from Harry's own manuscript (1976)

Chapter 4: The Glorious Years 1945-51

[This chapter of Harry's life, as it evolves at a remarkable pace, reflects an epic of truly heroic proportions, none of which Harry could have anticipated. But it is a mark of Harry's incredible versatility and leadership qualities that he could turn his experience as a pilot into serving as a secret emissary of David Ben Gurion, the head of the Jewish Agency for Palestine]

Harry returned to the Congo in late 1946 with his new wife and Annette. This was to be a short visit to settle his business affairs which, he thought, would take up to a year. There were no western-type schools near Kutu and Annette who was now seven years old had to receive lessons at home during that limited period. Harry was able, despite the difficulties of the past, to re-establish contact with his first wife, Rosette (Zus), her husband and his son Ben who had all returned to Leopoldville. During the war years they had moved to Elizabethville where Antoine Delporte was responsible for the security of the Katanga mines.

His work done, Harry returned with his family to Palestine at the end of 1947, again closing the sawmill, perhaps forever.

As he had previously promised Yehuda Arazi, he immediately joined the Haganah. His arrival coincided with the vote in the General Assembly of the United Nations on 29 November 1947, in favour of the partition of Palestine into Jewish and Arab States. This favourable decision for the Yishuv, the Jewish community in Palestine, immediately galvanised David Ben Gurion, the Chairman of the Jewish Agency for Palestine, into preparing for a war with Arabs both inside and outside Palestine, who would attempt to thwart the UN decision.

Ben Gurion's major concern was the Haganah's lack of heavy weapons with which to confront regular Arab forces .He anticipated that they would invade across Palestine's borders once the British left in May. He called a few Haganah officers with experience in dealing with foreign governments and sent them on a shopping expedition for modern armaments. Among them were Ehud Avriel and Yehuda Arazi. Besides the lack of artillery and armour, another major weakness was the non-existence of an air force.

This was where Harry's previous RAF service, knowledge of foreign languages and pure audacity, could be put to good use. He thus became one of the founding members of the secret air service, the" *Sherut Ha'Avir"*, with special responsibility for aircraft procurement in Europe. In addition, he would have to find pilots to fly any planes acquired to Palestine and provide, where necessary, training facilities for them. He received his instructions from Ben Gurion in person. The goal was to acquire war surplus aircraft, which could be converted to combat use once they were brought to Palestine. His first port of call was to be his old hunting ground, England.

Under his previous rank of Fl/Lt. H.G. Tursz-Fredkens in the Polish Air Force, he was nominated as the accredited representative of the Jewish Agency. On 5 December, prior to his departure from Palestine, he was given a note from Ben Gurion addressed to Joseph Linton, the Secretary-General of the London branch of the Agency. In the note Ben Gurion indicated that the treasurer of the Agency in Israel, Joseph Kaplan would make available $20 million for aircraft purchases

He requested that all assistance be given to Harry and that he be introduced to *"our friends":* Zigmund Gestetner and Sir Simon Marks. These were all prominent Jewish businessmen.

To provide additional cover for Harry, in case of later difficulty with the British or other authorities, the Haganah thought it wise that he also possessed another identity. He was therefore furnished with the name of Julius Lewis, a Canadian pastry chef, born in 1917.

After his arrival in London, Harry was put in contact with W.S. Shackleton Ltd, the biggest dealers in used aircraft in Europe. Over the next weeks he purchased several obsolete wooden aircraft of pre-war design and low performance, which, on the face of it, could only be used for training purposes. Harry also signed a contract for the training of 24 pilots who would be flying these aircraft.

In order to obtain permission from the Air Ministry to fly certain types of aircraft across Britain, Harry passed a medical fitness test on 19 December 1947. This was necessary to renew his Pilot's Licence and Certificate of Competency, which had expired in March whilst he was still in the Congo. He gave his address as Stratford Court Hotel, 350 Oxford Street, London, W.1 The very next day, using a fair measure of *"Chutspah",* Harry then obtained similar documents in the name of Julius Lewis. For this false document he used one of his younger looking photographs. This time he gave his address as the Regent's Palace Hotel, Piccadilly.

He now had two separate identities which he could use at will, depending on the role he needed to play: Flight Lieutenant or pastry chef.

Harry renewed his contact with Dan Tolkovski, who had been a fighter pilot with the Royal Rhodesian Air Force during the war. After being demobilized, Dan was working in Slough in an engineering company.

Interviewed at the age of 86, Dan recalls Harry's phone call in December 1947:

"I quickly recognised his characteristic accent when speaking English. It was sort of cosmopolitan/Jewish. When we later met, and Harry told me of his need for pilots, I immediately chucked my job in!"

He described Harry as an adventurer in every sense of the word, *"A colourful guy"*. Dan's first job for Harry was to fly a Tiger Moth from Oxford to London. In a later assignment he was to pick up a Proctor from the Toussus-Le-Noble civilian airfield outside Paris and fly it to Rome on its way to Palestine. Unfortunately, in Rome Dan was hit by the aircraft's propeller, badly fracturing his arm. He therefore had to remain temporarily in Rome, his arm encased in plaster.

By 28 December, Aharon Remez, ,later to be appointed Commander of the IAF, and Alex Zieloni of "*Sherut Ha'Avir*" could report to Ben Gurion that *"Freddy"*, as Harry was known, had acquired eight Tiger moths, three Avro Ansons, two Proctors and one Auster. The next problem was to acquire the necessary export licences to enable them to be despatched to Palestine. It was at this juncture that the Foreign Office intervened. It instructed the Ministry of supply to withhold export licences for these aircraft together with the engines and spare parts which had also been acquired. The British Government was determined to block the supply of any equipment, which might have a military use in Palestine, then still under their control[5]

In a letter to the Ministry of Supply in January 1948, the Shackleton directors protested this embargo, pointing out that Fl/Lt. Tursz-Fredkens was commissioned by the Jewish Agency for Palestine to purchase civilian and military aircraft and equipment to a value of £4 million.

"for the State of Palestine, wherever they may be available" It was also noted that *"Fl/Lt. Fredkens prefers to buy British because of his association with the RAF, and also on account of the fact that almost all Jewish pilots,*

---

[5] F.6. A letter from the Treasury Solicitor on 3 August 1948 mentions Fredkens as a suspected conspirator .

air crew and ground personnel had experience and training with British aircraft and engines"[6]

They hinted that, although British equipment was preferred, aircraft were available in other countries should export licences not be granted. These pleas fell on deaf ears and Harry, always full of ingenuity, then found an alternative solution. If export licences for Palestine were not available, then a new destination would be found. Within a short time, an *"Australian company"* showed an interest in acquiring some of Harry's aircraft for crop-spraying purposes, delivery to be made in Singapore. On this basis, export licences were granted for five Avro Anson and they were flown to Paris in February. Harry followed on a scheduled flight as by now his stay in the UK was becoming, by the day, more precarious. In Paris he had hoped to meet up with Ehud Avriel, but he was in Prague at the time negotiating an important arms deal. So, not to be delayed in his tasks, Harry flew off to Tel Aviv.

On 27 February 1948, three days after he left London, Ben Gurion recorded in his war diary, *"Freddy"* reported to him in person on his accomplishments. In total he had sent out of England five Ansons, one Rapide and one Proctor. There were still six Tiger Moths and four Amphibious planes left in England. They were being repaired but would be able leave in four to six weeks. Ben Gurion, however, was aware that the British had imposed an embargo on the supply of planes to the Middle East, so the likelihood of their leaving England was in some doubt.

Harry indicated to Ben Gurion that he now wished to go to the Congo for two weeks to sort out his affairs and see his son. Ben Gurion agreed if Harry would first provide him with a full report on the needs of a future Air Force and a summary of *"What we are [presently] doing wrong"*. Ben Gurion also asked that planes be kept in

---

[6] N.A FO371/68646

Europe, either in France or Italy until the British left Palestine on 15 May. In Ben Gurion's war diaries *"Freddy"* is mentioned at least twenty times.

Back in the Congo, Harry met up with Alfons Vandecasteele, his sister's husband, who had arrived in Kutu in 1947 to run Harry's sawmill. After his liberation from a concentration camp, Alfons was unable to return to the navy as he had lost the sight of one eye. As Harry knew he wasn't earning much working in a factory, he had suggested that he acts as his agent in the Congo, whilst Harry was otherwise occupied. If this worked out, his family could then join him. Unhappily for Alfons, it was to take another two years before he was finally reunited with his family.

As soon as Harry re-emerged in Paris, in the second part of March, he was commissioned to prepare another operation of even greater significance than his first mission in England. At this point he was supplied by Reuven Shiloah the head of the Hagana's secret service, with the real Julius Lewis's actual passport issued by the Canadian authorities. As the passport contains a tourist visa issued by the French consulate in Toronto on 23 February for a 10 day stay, one could speculate that, having arrived at Le Havre on 14 March, the real Lewis was transiting through France on his way to join an illegal boat to Palestine. No doubt, as this genuine passport was now destined for Harry's own use, Lewis handed it over to a local Haganah officer. By the time Harry received the passport a few days later the description page, except for the date of birth, had been suitably amended to incorporate his own details, such as height, colour of eyes and hair. On the third page was a recent photo of Harry carefully over stamped in one corner with *"Dept. of External Affairs- Canada"*. Below was the signature *"J.Lewis"* in Harry's own handwriting. All in all, the passport had been beautifully forged, except for one detail. The fact that Harry was 42 years old at the time, whilst Lewis, according to the date of birth in the passport, was only 30. This anomaly, which should have been obvious from Harry's photograph, seems to have escaped the attention of immigration officers across Europe during the actual six months of the passport's use.

When Harry met Ehud Avriel and Shaul Me'irov, the head of *"The Mossad l'Aliyah Bet"* (Illegal immigration organisation), during his stay in Paris, they gave him clear instructions as to his new task. He was to charter a large transport plane with which to fly badly needed automatic weapons from Czechoslovakia to Palestine. An anecdote related in Dominique Lapierre's book *"O Jerusalem"* suggests that, quite by chance, *"Julius"* met an American aircraft crew of Ocean Trade Airways in the Hotel California and that they subsequently accepted his invitation to dinner at the *"Jour et Nuit"*. There Harry revealed to them his identity as a Haganah officer and proposed to charter their DC4 Skymaster for the exorbitant sum of $10,000 for a round trip, Paris/Prague/Palestine/Prague. They quickly accepted as this was far more profitable than their current business of smuggling nylon stockings and cigarettes into Europe. This anecdote is generally corroborated, as the British Embassy in Prague reported the landing at the airport on 31 March of a Skymaster number 58201, with American markings. A large cargo of seven tons was loaded under the supervision of the Czech police and the plane took off. When the crew were interviewed the following day on their return, they stated that they had flown *"surgical instruments and small tools"* to Palestine and had landed at 10.30 PM at the old RAF airfield at Beit Daras (35 miles South West of Jerusalem). After unloading they left two hours later for Prague. A certain Mr. Cooper [Ami Cooperman, a former Canadian Air Force pilot employed by Harry] had accompanied the flight since it left Paris.[7] Thus was

---

[7] N.A FO 371/68635.

completed *" Balak 1"*, a joint operation between Harry in Europe and Aharon Remez, then planning officer of " *Sherut Ha'Avir"* in Palestine

The High Commissioner in Palestine confirmed the landing in Beit Daras to the Foreign Office on 7 April. He indicated that flares along the disused runway had been set up by members of a local Jewish settlement and that carts to take away the cargo were already on site an hour before the plane landed.[8]

We now know that the cargo comprised 100 heavy machine guns and ammunition which were used 5 days later for" *Operation Nachshon"*, a Haganah offensive to open the road to Jerusalem. The weapons were an essential requirement for the success of the operation. For months, since the Partition Vote in New York, Arab irregulars had managed to cut off supplies on the only passable road to Jerusalem. The Haganah with mostly small arms at their disposal were unable to break through, given the superior numbers of the enemy, well entrenched in the hills overlooking the road. This was the first time that the Haganah operated as a brigade force comprising 1500 men. The operation in the Latrun area cleared the mountain road to Jerusalem allowing Palmach trucks to deliver supplies to the beleaguered city, at least for a short period. Harry had been instrumental in pulling off a remarkable feat, but most of the credit went to Ehud Avriel who had succeeded in acquiring the arms in the first place. Harry's contribution was only recognised much later thanks to a few paragraphs in *"O, Jerusalem"*.

In early April, whilst he was still in Paris, a new and urgent task awaited Harry, which could not be delayed. He was instructed to attempt to sink a ship which had sailed on 31 March from the Adriatic port of Fiume and which was heading for Beirut. The Haganah were aware from their sources in Prague that the ship, the Lino, contained a

---

[8] N.A FO 371/68635

cargo of 10,000 rifles and ammunition purchased in Czechoslovakia for the Syrian army. Harry proposed to use for the mission one of the Ansons parked at the Toussus-le-Noble Airfield. This twin-engine aircraft designed initially as a coastal-patrol land-plane, had been used by the RAF at the beginning of the war for anti-submarine duties and could carry a heavy bombload in the centre section. Its disadvantages were that it was slow, cold and noisy. To a veteran pilot like Harry, who had flown anything from bi-planes to Wellington bombers these were insignificant problems. As to the bombs, Harry had these in two suitcases, which he just managed to haul on board. His first stop would be Rome, where local Haganah agents would supply him with his latest instructions. For three days in succession, and in possession of very precise details of the boat's speed and direction, Harry flew up and down the Adriatic and eventually spotted the boat. However, it was a fruitless task. In the absence of bomb racks, Harry's plan, to attach the bombs to cables from the aircraft and drop them with precision onto the deck, proved technically impossible. Harry's brief mission had come to an end and he left the Anson at Rome airport. The Lino was eventually sunk by Palestinian frogmen in the port of Bari on the night of 9/10 April.

Now for the first time, Harry used his forged Julius Lewis passport. An inspection of that passport reveals an incredible number of entry stamps between April to September 1948 covering a myriad of countries across Europe. He seemed to be driven by the urgency of acquiring the necessary equipment for Israel to defend itself. A few details reflect the trail he followed:

First, Harry flew to Paris on 3 April and obtained a tourist visa for Italy. He then flew to Geneva to pick up new instructions from his Haganah controller and then proceeded to Rome. Here he picked up Dan's Proctor and flew it to Brussels. On 4 April, Ben Gurion noted in his war diary that in Brussels, Harry had bought 31 artillery cannons located in Denmark. Subsequently on 12 April, Ben Gurion noted that Freddy had bought 29 single-engine Norseman planes in Germany. These light transport planes were to be used for transferring supplies to outlying kibbutzim in Palestine. They could carry at least seven people plus supplies and were being sold by the American Office of the Foreign Liquidation Commissioner. Harry bought them at a base near Munich at a price of $12,000 each. On 16 April, following this transaction, Harry obtained a visa for Denmark, which he visited between the 17 and 18 April to inspect his cannon purchases. He then flew himself back to the small airfield of Toussus-Le-Noble. Having obtained a new visa, Harry left for Italy and was in Rome the next evening. He rested for two weeks from his galivanting across Europe, whilst he planned on how to effect delivery of the Norseman planes to Palestine.

In the meantime, the Ansons had left Paris for Rome. On this leg of the journey one crash-landed outside Milan and came to the attention of British Intelligence. With the knowledge that the next refuelling stop would be the Greek island of Rhodes, the British alerted the local authorities that the pilots were suspected communists. When, on 10 April, the other four planes arrived they were immediately impounded, and the pilots and passengers detained.

According to newspaper reports, the pilots were Horace Mann, Leonard Cohen, Hubert Curtis and Dan Tolkovski. Although Dan was on one of the planes, he was merely a passenger. He had been picked up in Rome, his arm still in plaster, when the planes landed there for a refuelling stop. After a month of house arrest in a local hotel where they were interrogated by a British police mission from Palestine, Dan, the only Palestinian amongst them, was released. He flew off via Athens to Lydda. Apparently, Colonel Prosser, the Senior British police officer had told his Greek counterpart that he knew Dan's parents and therefore he couldn't possibly be a communist. A few days later, the pilots and the other passengers were also released, but the planes remained in Rhodes until the Arab/Israeli conflict ended in 1949. A report in the National Archives signed by the Treasury Solicitor in August 1948 reveals that, as a result of Harry's involvement in this affair and that of an ex-RAF sergeant called Freddy Friedman they were both sought by the police for infringements of the provisions of the Air Navigation Order. [9]

In the meantime, and without Harry's knowledge, Ben Gurion, in keeping with his usual secretive habits, had already commissioned another agent to work in England. This was Emanuel Zur (Zuckerberg), chief pilot of the Palestinian civilian Aviron Aviation Company.[10] When Zur, with the CID at his tail, also had to decamp quickly to Paris, he appointed, in his stead, a non-Jewish Briton called Terence Farnfield. It was this ex-RAF pilot who, despite the embargo, was instrumental in arranging the disappearance from England of two Mosquitos in July 1948 and four Beaufighters in August. A letter to the British Colonial Office on 23.9.48 states:

"4 Beaufighters left Thame Airport, Haddenham, Bucks on 1 August .These aircraft were not airworthy and were flown on forged certificates to Ajaccio, Corsica and from there to Palestine. The Ministry of Aviation was tricked by a pretence on the part of a gentleman called Farnfield that he was shooting a film for which he required Beaufighters. The aircraft were given permission to fly to the scene of the film (Exeter) and did not appear again"[11]

RAF photo reconnaissance identified these 4 planes at Aqir, Palestine on 5 August. Similarly, the 2 Mosquitos

---

[9] N.A F.6
[10] N.A E6484
[11] N.A FO.371/68638

were identified by the RAF on 10 August at Ramat David[12].

Whilst the pilots of the Beaufighters later received light fines for their escapade, the actual aircraft dealer, Harold Towle, was sentenced in 1950 to six months imprisonment and a fine of £2,500 for the illegal export of just one of the Mosquitos. (The Times, 23.12.1950). It is tempting to speculate just what sentence Harry might have faced if he had been caught by the police at the time. In any event, he was not to revisit England until 1961. But this time, he was protected by an Israeli diplomatic passport. He intended to visit Tursz family members in Blackpool.

In Rome, Harry had established his base at a local hotel and set about recruiting pilots. He brought Ida over from Tel Aviv to release him from an increasing burden of administrative tasks. Annette related to me an anecdote from her mother: Once, when Harry returned to the hotel from one of his trips, the reception clerk drew him quietly to one side and reported that his wife (Ida Tursz-Fredkens) was receiving numerous calls from a *"Major Lewis"* who spoke to her in a very strange language. This in fact was the pseudonym Harry used, whenever he had to contact Ida on one of his trips. In case he was being overheard, the language they spoke was Lingala, a Congolese dialect.

Another anecdote refers to a trip made by Ida and Harry to Paris at that time. It was to be the first occasion since her departure from Paris in 1945 that Ida could re-establish contact with the Szwarc family. This was to include my mother and myself, now resident there. Also, it was an opportunity for all to become acquainted with Harry. [Personally, I do not recall that visit]. Ida told my mother that, before Paris, she attempted to visit London. Despite her French passport (Her parents were naturalised

---

[12] N.A FO.371/68638

in 1939) she did not proceed further than the Immigration Authorities .The surname, Tursz-Fredkens, was on a wanted list and she was grilled by the police as to Harry's whereabout. Her refusal to answer their questions led to her being refused entry into the UK. She then re-joined Harry in Paris.

So much for anecdotes.

The Norseman planes were flown either to Shiphol Airport near Amsterdam or Toussus-Le-Noble, where twelve-hour long-range fuel tanks were fitted, in preparation for their flight to Palestine. By the end of April, five of the planes were ready at Shiphol and at Toussus-Le-Noble. Three were flown to Rome via Marseilles and Nice and experienced some technical difficulties. On 19 May, Harry held a briefing meeting with seven aircrew at the hotel in Rome. Among them were Leonard Cohen, newly released from Rhodes and the famous fighter ace, George Beurling, formerly of the Canadian Royal Air force. Two days later, Harry launched test flights by flying one of the Norsemans himself with two of the crew. The next to attempt a test flight were Cohen and Beurling. Unfortunately, Beurling carried out air acrobatics above the airport which the plane was not designed for. The plane caught fire and dived into the ground. Both pilots were killed. Harry had to use all his persuasive powers to reassure the other pilots that the reserve tanks on the Norsemans were safe. He emphasised how important it was to bring the planes to Israel as soon as possible. One hour after the crash four of the pilots flew the other two planes to Brindisi en- route for Palestine. Because of Beurling's fame the crash in Rome was widely reported in the International press.

Back in April, Ben Gurion had appointed one of the most experienced former-RAF officers, Yehoshua Gilutz, as Controlling Air Officer-Europe to be based in Rome. And so, yet another emissary was inserted into the aircraft and pilot procurement circuit. Was Ben Gurion hedging his bets or was this an example of a scatter-gun approach to the problem of the lack of an adequate air force? In the event Gilutz arrived in Zurich carrying a slip of paper addressed to Shaul Avigur (formerly Me'irov) to release $2 million to him to purchase aircraft. As Gilutz now relates, Avigur welcomed him from his sick–bed and questioned the necessity of providing the funds. It should be noted that Avigur was one of the few people in the Mapai (Labour Party) hierarchy who could choose to ignore Ben Gurion's instructions if he felt so inclined. Gilutz's response to Avigur's prevarications was to ask for an immediate yes or no answer. As it was not forthcoming, he indicated his intention to return immediately to Tel Aviv. In retrospect, Gilutz understood that Avigur, at the time, was still supporting Harry's own endeavours in Europe and saw no need for yet another player in the field.

On 20 May Ben Gurion noted in his diary that Avigur recommended that Harry be relieved of his duties as central organiser for aircraft procurement in Europe. A few days later Ya'akov Dori, the Commander of all Israeli forces, recommended the repatriation of both Harry and Ami Cooperman to Israel. One can speculate that the failure of the Anson operation led to this decision. Later in August 1948, Avigur recommended to Ben Gurion, that Harry should cease handling aircraft procurement altogether.

Harry, nevertheless, continued to supervise the movement of the Norseman planes to Israel and on one occasion piloted one of the planes himself. Flying at night in the Nice area he had to make a crash landing. After ending up in some trees, the co-pilot managed to get out of the plane, but Harry was knocked unconscious, with severe head injuries. An hour later he was extracted from the plane by French paratroopers from a nearby base and taken to hospital. There he underwent an operation, which involved placing a silver plate in his temple. He made a slow but successful recovery. In later years, though, he was to complain of amnesia and absent-mindedness. From June to September Harry kept up his remorseless Proctor flights between, Paris, Brussels, Amsterdam and Geneva. On 23 July he made a trip to Prague in connection with the ongoing training of Palestinian pilots on Spitfires, provided by the Czechoslovakian air Force.

In September 1948 his return to Israel after an 11-hour flight from Brindisi, via Greece, leading a group of four of the Norsemans, was witnessed by Annette and the crowd as they flew over the Tel Aviv seashore to the Sde Dov airfield. Strangely enough, Harry had obtained an immigrant's visa from the Israeli Consulate in Paris before his departure. He therefore entered Israel as a new immigrant under the false name of Julius Lewis. Nonetheless, this marked the temporary end to Harry's adventures in Europe and he reverted to his proper name. Back in February 1948, because of his outstanding service in the Haganah, he had been appointed a full colonel in *"Sherut Ha'Avir"* and he carried this rank into the IAF when it was created in May. Initially Harry was stationed at the Air Force Headquarters in the Yarkon Hotel. His next appointment was as Forward Air Controller attached to Yitzhak Sadeh's 8th armoured brigade in the Negev desert. His call sign was *"Tester 5"*. From his Piper Cub he directed Harvard advanced trainers, converted to dive bombers, onto the Egyptian lines.

He was also credited with designing search lights, placed under aircraft which helped to pinpoint targets in the Egyptians' Faluja position, which was then heavily bombarded.

In January 1949, Harry was present when four RAF Spitfires on a photo-reconnaissance mission over the Egyptian/Israeli border were shot down by the IAF. He interrogated one of the two surviving pilots, Timothy McElhaw, promising him an early grave if he didn't cooperate. The other pilot, Frank Close, who suffered from a broken jaw and concussion during his parachute landing, later asserted at an RAF enquiry in Cairo that, during the first six days of his stay in hospital, he was:

"severely grilled by intensive questioning, usually twice a day."[13] [By Harry?]

After this incident Harry was concerned that the pilots might have identified him as an ex-RAF officer. This was a further reason for him not to contemplate a visit to England for the foreseeable future. At the time, the shooting down of the four British Spitfires and a Tempest in a later dogfight was a controversial issue between the British and the Israeli Provisional Government, as two pilots lost their lives. The main issue was whether the 5 planes had been shot down over Egyptian or Israeli territory. Later historical accounts make it quite clear that Israeli forces at the time had made an incursion into Egyptian territory and did not want their positions revealed. Any non-Israeli aircraft flying over this area were therefore considered hostile and were engaged in combat. Ezer Weizman was one of the Israeli pilots involved in the second dogfight, when a large flight of Tempest RAF planes flew over the area in search of the four missing Spitfires. This was when David Tattersfield, a Tempest pilot was shot down and killed. He was buried with full military honours in the British cemetery in Ramle. An attempt many years later to bring together the pilots from both sides in a reconciliation reunion in Israel failed, only because of the opposition of Ezer Weizman, for reasons best known to himself.

After the cessation of combat with the Arab forces in mid-1949, Harry in company with other IAF officers, was able to acquire a plot of land in an under-developed area of

---

[13] N.A Air 19/587

Tel Aviv. It was called *"Schechounot Ha'Katzinim"* ("Officers' housing quarter"). Ben Gurion was present at its official opening.

It was around about this time that Harry proved to be a guardian angel to my French cousin Maurice.[14]

Harry's tasks in the IAF until 1951 remain unclear, but a contemporary of his, Colonel Yehoshua Gilutz, does not recall ever seeing him in uniform during that period. Harry relates mysteriously, in one of his later letters, that nothing much would be found in his personal file for that period, when his boss was Aharon Remez. This is

---

[14] Maurice Szwarc, my cousin, came to Israel from Paris on his 18th birthday in May 1948. He had signed an agreement with the French branch of "Machal" (Volunteers from outside Israel) that he would serve in the Israeli Army until the end of hostilities with the Arab States. He was enrolled in the "*Palmach*" (Israel's shock troops) until April 1949 and then, like others in his *"Machal"* group, wished then to be demobilized in accordance with the agreement. But this became a drawn-out affair and the process was very slow. In August 1949 Maurice with his comrade Armand, marched into the offices of the French "*Machal*" and made their demands clear. But to no avail, as the Director, Pierre Mouchenik, refused to let them jump the queue.

Maurice, in despair, went to see his aunt Ida in Tel Aviv, appealing for help. Within days, Colonel Harry Fredkens , in full IAF uniform, accompanied Maurice and Armand on a new visit to the Director's office Using the authority of his rank, Harry bellowed in English *"I know these men and they must be liberated now!"*.

My cousin, who related this story, showed me a copy of a declaration, dated 22 August from Mouchenik. It confirmed *that "Szwarc Maurice-No.Mle. 60913"* was demobilized back-dated to 21 April 1949. This clearly shows how effective Harry's intervention had been.

Maurice and Armand rejoined their group on Kibbutz .Maurice was to stay In Israel until 1953 when he returned to Paris with Ruthi, his wife. Maurice is now 89 years old and is still going strong. He just loves to be interviewed!

confirmed in a letter from Remez to Arik Sharon, the Defence Minister in 1983. He specifically states that much of Harry's activities in this period were not adequately documented but that this in no way diminished his services to the State.

On leaving the IAF in September 1951 on extended leave and with a 32% disability pension, Harry took Ida and Annette back to the Congo. He was not to return permanently to Israel for the next 8 years. In September 1953 he officially left the IAF, but retained his rank of colonel

For Harry these had been the *"glorious years"*. He was proud of his clandestine achievements, carried out selflessly for the State of Israel. Much later he was to bemoan the fact that others did not adequately recognise this.

Ida checking her yellow star outside the block where she lived with Annette and her mother-in-law.

[The wearing of the yellow Star in Paris by adult Jews was made compulsory by the Gestapo in June 1942]

Ida and Annette arriving in Haifa, 1945

Harry (on the left) and Ida (on the right) in October 1946 some time after their marriage

Harry's visit to Coutrai, Belgium in early 1946 to visit his sister Ralla and her family. Here he is in the background with Ralla, his nephew Georges on the right and his niece Doris on the left.

Harry and Ralla

Harry with Ida, Annette and their dog outside the saw-mill at Kutu in early 1947 after their arrival from Mandate Palestine

Aboard the *"Louisette"* at Kutu. Annette aged 8 is seated on the floor of the boat. Harry is seated to the left and Ida is seated on the right.

Ida and Harry in 1948 on a short visit to Paris from Rome. At the time they were both working for the Haganah

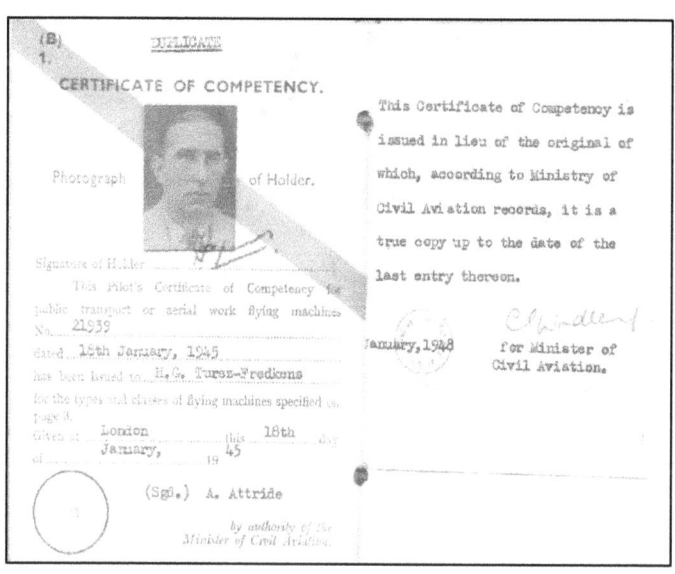

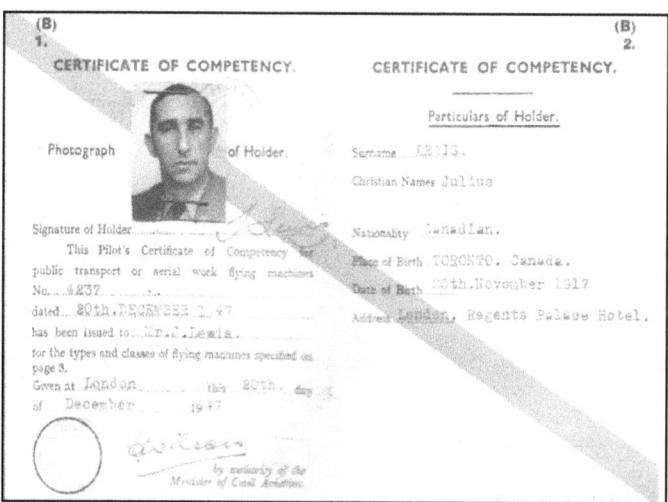

The first Certificate of Competency (dated 1945) is genuine, whilst the second (dated 1947) was obtained by deception using the name Julius Lewis

Harry's forged Canadian passport in the name of Lewis

Harry on Far left

The official opening, in the presence of the Prime Minister, David ben Gurion and his wife, of a project to house IAF officers and their families.

Chapter 5: The second Belgian Congo venture 1951-1959

[This new period in Harry's life was to bring great wealth as his timber business prospered under Belgian colonial rule. He became very profligate and enjoyed all the privileges of an expatriate. However, interviews with his sister's children and Ben his son, revealed certain traits of his character which were not very endearing. The chapter ends with the coming of Congolese independence and Harry's reluctant decision to abandon his business and return to Israel, where an uncertain future awaited him]

In 1951, after his temporary discharge from the IAF, Harry decided that his best prospect for the future lay with his business activities in the Congo. Accompanied by Ida and Annette he arrived back at Kutu in September to be welcomed by his sister Ralla and her family. In April 1949 Ralla had finally re-joined her husband with Clare, but Doris and Georges did not come until December 1950

Harry quickly renewed his pilot's licence with the Belgian Congolese authorities, but this time as an Israeli citizen. At Kutu there was no missionary school, so Annette was sent to join Ralla's two daughters as a boarder at the Athene Royale secondary school in Leopoldville, which was run for expatriates by the Catholic Church. Jewish girls were excused from attending religious services.

After Harry's return, Ben started to come from Leopoldville to Kutu during school holidays and later from Belgium, during university vacations. On those occasions, he went hunting and fishing with his father. Harry taught him mathematics and trigonometry. This left Ben with a love of astronomy and navigation for the rest of his life

Ida was now still only 32 years old, but she decided not to have any children with Harry. She felt that as Harry already had his son and that she had a daughter, it would only lead to complications in the future if they had children together. Harry, despite his desire for more children accepted the position with good grace. For him there was no conflict in his affection for both Ben and Annette. He loved them both dearly. Annette certainly returned his affection but Ben, after the end of his university studies, could only admire him from afar. Their meetings in the future would be infrequent, given their different career paths and locations. Always overshadowing their relationship was Harry's perceived off-hand treatment of Ben's mother, Rosette, before the war.

For Ben, Harry remained the most fascinating of men until the end of his days, despite his misgivings about some of his later business ventures and the cavalier way he treated people. Ben's few meetings with Harry were always welcome. They were never planned, for Ben, tended to be abroad on extended periods on his academic pursuits. Often they met over a copious restaurant meal which they both liked to indulge in. *"Le Boeuf sur le Toit"* in Brussels was one of their favourite venues. The menu included crocodile meat, which they had learnt to eat in the Congo whilst in the bush with the natives.

Claire first remembers seeing Harry at her parent's house, where with a Mr. Chevaux, who worked for Harry, they played cards nearly every night. As to Georges, his recollections are of being with his sisters and Harry's son, Ben at the Athene Royale. In 1953 when Harry and his family had moved to a beautiful villa at Djelo-Binza, in Leopoldville, Doris, who was now 19, stayed with them. Claire recalled being picked up by Doris every Saturday from the boarding school and spending her weekends at the villa where she saw Annette and played with the family dog.

In 1956, a year after Claire had finished at the boarding school, Ralla and Alphons also came to live in Djelo-Binza. Apparently, they had fallen out with Harry, presumably over money affairs and Alfons was no longer working for him. Claire mentioned family arguments and that her mother no longer wished to see her brother.

Annette now 16 and thoroughly sick of her years of residence at the Athene Royale asked Harry and Ida to let her go to Israel to finish her education. There she would be looked after by Ida's sisters. Recognising that this was the right course for Annette, they regretfully let her go. She was never to return to the Congo.

Sometime later, Harry suggested another job for Alphons which would involve him leaving home and working in the field, seeking out good timber. However, this project also came to an unsatisfactory end and Alphons returned to Leopoldville. This was to be Ralla and Alphons's last contact with Harry as they never forgave him for letting them down a second time.

When I asked about their recollections of Harry, both Claire and Georges felt that he had duped their father and mother with offers of well-paid jobs which came to nothing. On the other hand, Claire added that Harry was a big man who liked to laugh and had a great sense of humour. Always at ease in public. Regaling people with jokes, Harry was a great organiser, and this impinged on other peoples' lives. According to Georges, he was also a great entrepreneur who built a whole series of villas at Binza, below Djelo-Binza. He was characterised as cunning and, according to people who had dealings with him, somewhat underhand in business matters.

At one time Harry employed some 500 natives and, although he was a difficult and demanding taskmaster, they respected him for his technical skills. When I told Ben that Harry was, according to Annette's memory, referred to as *"Le Bon Blanc" ("The good white man")* he did his best to dissuade me from that idea. He stated categorically that Harry was a racist and could be exceedingly harsh towards those natives he did not favour. Those he did favour like Jules the cook and Mamadu, who ran the furnaces, he could be very generous to. It all depended on his mood. He was prone to irrational and uncontrolled fits of temper with those who crossed him. Ben himself witnessed Harry beating a village chief with a stick, because he had allegedly cheated him over some transaction. In Ben's view this negative side of Harry's temperament was no different from that of the other expatriates in the Congo. Apartheid in all walks of life had been imposed in the Belgian Congo well before that in South Africa.

Ben's friend *"Mac"* from Brussels was far less harsh in his judgement of Harry. He hadn't known Harry in those days but surmised that Harry was the type to have a *"joking relationship with the natives".* Does all this indicate the attitude of a bully or, conversely, a truly paternalistic approach to his workers?

The routine at Kutu followed a regular pattern. Every morning at 9 AM there was *"Appel"* for the first 8-hour shift in the sawmill, at which the natives were counted and allotted their tasks for the day. It was important, in view of tribal and other sensitivities, to ensure that the teams were able to work harmoniously together. Ben preferred to take the early shift. At other times, he would fly over the 30,000 hectares concession with Harry to pinpoint the next area to be cut down. On his return to Kutu he would then cross Lake Leopold II and, with a skilled lumberjack began the long trek on foot to the new site at the rate of some 15 kilometres a day. Ben reckoned that a high yield productivity would be to cut down some 40 to 50 cubic metres of trees per hectare. The next task was to move the logs to the riverbank at the Lukenie, which was never more than two days march away. For this, tractors were brought into the forest. In view of the lack of turning space, the tractors after arrival would reverse pulling the logs behind them until they reached the shore. It was on the shore of the Lukenie that the massive logs (sometimes their radius was the height of a man) were roped together with chains. This created a raft of some 1000 cubic metres which was floated down river over a period of days into Lac Leopold II. Two or three men sat on the raft but could not steer it. Once the raft reached Ebabaka adjacent to Lake Leopold II, a tug would set off from the other side of the lake at Kutu to bring it in. This happened every two weeks or so.

At Kutu, the problem was to bring the logs to the sawmill. This was achieved by digging out a ditch into which a long trailer was placed. As a log was dragged onto the trailer from the shore, an ex-army Ford lorry was attached to the trailer, which pulled it out of the ditch with its load. This process was repeated until the whole 1000 cubic metres was brought to the sawmill. As always, Harry's ingenuity found answers to the most difficult of technical problems. The choice of Kutu as the location for the sawmill, directly opposite the Lukenie River was equally not a chance decision, but a well calculated move.

At the mill a good month's production of sawn timber would be some 500 to 700 cubic metres. At today's values this represented a monthly turnover of some $500,000. The net profit to Harry, given the very low cost of labour, was some $150,000 per month By any stretch of the imagination, Harry should have been a very rich man in those days. But, as Ben relates, he was a big spender and to own the only Jaguar car in Leopoldville and a several light aircraft was the way Harry liked to portray himself to the other expatriates. Holidays in South Africa were also de rigueur. Harry always believed he had *"Baraka"* a term often used in Africa meaning good luck

When in 1957 Ben married in Brussels, in the presence of his mother and Antoine Delporte, Harry did not attend. Instead he sent Annette from Israel to represent him. Harry's relationship with Edith, Ben's wife was not very warm and when later he accused her of being after his money, she was mortally offended. Ben, despite an active academic career, he was professor in the Animal Biology Department of Brussels University, was virtually Harry's agent in Europe obtaining for him tractors and other industrial equipment for the sawmill. This close business association between father and son was to continue through many years despite their frequent and lengthy geographical separations and differences of outlook.

It will be recalled that Belgium had run the Congo under a fair degree of paternalistic colonialism and racial segregation since 1908. Subsequently, the Belgian Government finally wrested this private fiefdom from the hands of Leopold II. Thereafter economic and social changes had transformed the Congo into a model colony. Hospitals and primary and high schools were built, and many Congolese had access to them. However, the educational system was dominated by the Catholic Church. Political administration fell under the direct control of Belgium as represented by its Governor General in Leopoldville. Already one of these incumbents in 1952 had warned that, unless native people were given more civil rights, even suffrage, Belgium would ultimately lose its richest colony.

There was little support for this view in Brussels despite pressure from the Soviet Union and the USA to reform its Congo policy in line with the United Nations Charter which advocated self-determination.

In 1955, demands for independence were mounting throughout Africa and the Congo was not immune to this.

Congolese nationalists like Joseph Kasavubu, who led the *"Alliance du Ba-Kongo (ABAKO)"* and Patrice Lumumba who led the *"Mouvement National Congolais (MNC)"* became increasingly strident for independence from the Belgians. Political unity, however, was complicated by ethnic rivalries among the native population. The Brussels government was particularly worried by Lumumba who advocated left-wing views and supported the idea of complete unity for the Congo on independence. This it saw as a threat to its financial interests in Katanga and Kasai where its copper, gold and diamond activities were situated.

After the Leopoldville riots in March 1959, all Congolese political parties were legalised and this was followed by general elections. The results reflected both the strong influence of the MNC and the ethnic split as represented by the parties of Joseph Kasavubu (BaKongo), Joseph Kalonji (Kasai) and Moise Tschombe (Katanga).

Harry now foresaw that the major element of his sawmill venture, the availability of transport and particularly water transport would be seriously affected by social and political disruptions. He decided that the time had come to cut his losses and return to Israel with Ida. At this stage he was hedging his bets and didn't want his business to be sold. So, before he left, he appointed Adolphe Bapeke, the company's accountant, to maintain the business and report back to Harry regularly. This decision did not prove successful and eventually Harry managed to sell the business as a going concern to the Dutch Borneo-Sumatra Company at a good price. But this venture also failed and today the forest has reclaimed the site at Kutu.

By the end of 1959, the Belgians finally realised that their political hold on the Congo was fast diminishing and they therefore called a Round Table Conference with the Congolese political parties in Brussels .This was held in January 1960. A decision was then made to grant independence on 30 June. In the ensuing elections the high vote for ABAKO ensured that Kasavubu would be elected President whilst Lumumba would become Prime Minister of the newly independent state.

By now Harry was 55 and he was pondering how he would make a living in Israel to support himself, Ida and Annette. At the time Annette was completing a 3-year course in physiotherapy.

The Vandecasteele family in the Congo, starting from left:
Alfons, Doris, Georges, Ralla and Claire

Harry's house in Kutu with Alfons and Claire in the foreground

Ida in Leopoldville (1951)

A boat called *"Ida"* built by Harry and used as a tug.

Harry and Ben

Work at the sawmill supervised by Harry or Ben

Ida and Harry on the steps of their villa prior to their return to Israel in 1959

Chapter 6 Congolese politics before and after independence 1959-1961

[This chapter lays bare a fatal flaw in Harry's character, that of financial recklessness. Having gained the confidence of Congolese leaders, he allowed himself the luxury of believing that nothing was beyond his power to achieve. But when it came to the question of money-matters Harry, as he had shown in the past, was imprudent in the extreme. As later events were to show, Harry, in a foolhardy commitment, had planted the seeds of his ultimate financial downfall.]

By the time Harry returned to Israel he had dropped the name Harry Gregori Turz-Fredkens in all correspondence other than official documents, in favour of Colonel Harry Fredkens. This was, after all, the name he was known by, among his former IAF and Haganah colleagues in Israel.

Luckily for him, his homecoming coincided with the peak of French scientific cooperation with Israel over nuclear fission. His knowledge of French and his outgoing personality made him an ideal interlocutor with the French scientists, then working on the creation of a secret nuclear facility at Dimona in the Negev desert. His past activities on behalf of the State ensured that a suitable post was found for him as an engineer with CHAMAT. This organisation was partly responsible for the installation of the reactor on the building site and, for negotiating the cost of supplies with the French. According to his son, Harry's contribution was the design and construction of the dome, a series of rigid concrete triangles. In order to strengthen the concrete Harry devised a method whereby two metre length iron rods where literally fired into the still-soft concrete. This cheap construction method proved to be highly effective.

This leads us to an extraordinary narrative in Yediot Ahronot on 9 October 1992, entitled *"The Hit List"*. It was written by Shlomo Nakdimon, its political correspondent, and Eli Gingrich (later Eyal) a former IAF Lieutenant Colonel, who had grown attached to Harry in his later years. Although the historical background, that of the demise of Lumumba, the Prime Minister of the new Republic of the Congo, has been widely known from other sources, the details of Harry's own involvement, until then secret, were revealed by him to Eyal. This was no tall story as documents preserved by Harry and passed to Eyal substantially support Harry's narrative.

The story starts with Harry receiving a telephone call in early June 1960 whilst working at Dimona:

"This is Ehud Avriel speaking from the Foreign Office. Ben Gurion has given me the task of ambassador to the new Republic of the Congo and I invite you to join as one of the senior staff at the Embassy."

The Congo was to attain its independence from the Belgians on 30 June and the Israeli Government was keen to ensure its own diplomatic representation as it had been doing in other parts of Africa. Avriel had previously been ambassador to Ghana and Liberia and badly needed someone who was familiar with the Congo and its main political figures. This profile, Harry filled to perfection. To become an Israeli diplomat at his age despite his little knowledge of Hebrew, must have appeared to him as a God-sent opportunity to shine on a new stage. Without a moment's hesitation he accepted the appointment and broke the exciting news to Ida and Annette. He told them, however, that he couldn't take them with him. He didn't know at this stage how long the appointment would last, but risk-taker that he was, this was the least of his concerns. In his Zeitgeist, family and a stable employment would always take second place to the call of adventure.

Harry arrived with Ehud Avriel in the Congo on 27 June 1960 and was present a few days later, when Avriel, as Israel's first ambassador to the Republic of the Congo, presented his diplomatic credentials to President Kasavubu. After his stint in Ghana, where he had established a highly regarded reputation, Avriel had not been at all that keen on his new appointment. Nevertheless, he allowed himself to be persuaded by Ben Gurion, who described him as the only Israeli diplomat capable of helping the Congolese and in so doing the State of Israel.[15] This was a time when Nasser of Egypt was trying to wean away the African states from acquiring any economic or military assistance from Israel. In this he was abetted by the Soviet Union which, during the Cold War, viewed Israel as part of the Western Camp. Ben Gurion also had a strategic interest in maintaining good relations with the Congo. This was related to the supply of Uranium for the Dimona project, of which the Katanga province of the Congo had large deposits in addition to other minerals. The United States had already tapped into this source for the Manhattan Project in 1945. There is little doubt that the USA, Belgium and Israel had a common interest in preventing Lumumba's Marxist ideas dictating the orientation of politics in the Congo. Before the Israeli delegation left for the Congo, Ben Gurion visited Brussels to discuss with the Belgian Government the role Israel could play in the Congo. It is therefore quite conceivable that Harry was secretly tasked by Ben Gurion, through the Foreign Ministry, to assist Kasavubu, the designated President, towards the elimination of Lumumba as a political figure. Whether the term *"elimination"* in Harry's eyes, could also mean *"assassination"* is not substantiated in the documentation available. But the reality is that in January 1961, this is how Lumumba met his end.

---

[15] [15] Translation of Letter from Ben Gurion to Avriel dated 31 May 1960

As soon as Harry arrived in Leopoldville he searched out Congolese politicians whom he had known in former days. These included Maurice Mpolo, the Minister for Sport and Lutula, the Minister for Agriculture. Through their intermediary he was introduced firstly to Isaie Kuyena and Vital Moanda, both senior officials of *the "Alliance du Bas-Kongo" (ABAKO)* and then to President Joseph Kasavubu himself. Thereafter he visited Kasavubu at least once a week. To facilitate his entry to the President's Palace he was furnished with a special pass which assured him access without prior appointment.

The British Embassy in Tel Aviv was keen to keep the Foreign Office in London up to date on Israel's involvement in the Congo. In a despatch dated 21 June 1960, it noted that in addition to Ehud Avriel and Levi Eshkol, the Minister of Finance, the other members of the Israeli delegation would be;

"Mr.Moshe Pearlman and a certain Aluf-Mishne (Colonel) Fredkens... about Colonel Fredkens we know nothing, but one sentence in a Press report says that he has wide commercial contacts in the Congo. This leaves us more puzzled than before." [16]

Obviously, the fact that Harry was still on the police wanted list back in the UK was not common knowledge. In a later report dated 18 November, the British Consul in Leopoldville noted with satisfaction *that*:

"The Israelis began well in the Congo even including, much to the pleasure of the Congolese, a Lingala speaker in their delegation to the independence celebrations" [17]

Who else could this be, but Harry?

---

[16] N.A FO371/146761
[17] N.A FO371/146684

At the Independence day gathering on 30 June at which King Baudouin of Belgium presided, the cordial atmosphere was broken by Lumumba, who lambasted the Belgians for their colonial rule. He indicated that profound changes would be made to de-colonialise the Congo and ensure the unity of the new state, outside of ethnic considerations. This went down very badly with the local Belgian officers and civil servants present, although they kept their counsel at the time. The Belgian Government had viewed Congolese independence as a piece of window-dressing, which would not radically change the way the Congo had been run. They relied on Kasavubu's weakness in the political sphere to ensure his compliance. But Lumumba presented a real challenge to their aspirations and sooner or later he would have to be marginalized.

However, within days of independence, the *Force Publique* mutinied and refused to accept the orders of the white Belgian officers. Lumumba moved swiftly to fire the officers and appointed former colleagues, with some military experience, to run the now-renamed" *Armée Nationale Congolaise (ANC)*". Victor Lundula became Commander in Chief and Joseph Mobutu was promoted to colonel and became Chief of Staff. This was not the end of the troubles, for Katanga under Moise Tshombe seceded from the new republic, thus depriving it of a major part of its mineral wealth. Albert Kelonji later acted in a similar manner in south Kasai, the diamond-producing area.

Belgian citizens were abused by rampaging Congolese soldiers and the stories of atrocities provoked Brussels into flying in parachutists from Europe. Lumumba and Kasavubu called on the United Nations to react to this clear invasion of sovereignty. The first UN forces arrived on 15 July and under Lumumba's threat of seeking Soviet assistance, the Belgians agreed to withdraw their troops. A civil war erupted in various parts of the Congo as Lumumba struggled to end the secession of Katanga and south Kasai, each of which was defended by soldiers who had chosen ethnic loyalty over loyalty to the Republic.

The military campaign launched by Lumumba with those forces loyal to the central government caused widespread resentment, not least among the soldiers ordered to attack their own tribes. Politically, Lumumba was also losing support in his party, the MNC. It is at this point that Harry's story really takes off.

On 29 August Harry received an urgent telegram from Maurice Mpolo, the Minister for Youth and a principal colleague of Lumumba .This urged him to fly the next day to Inongo, on Lake Leopold II, to meet him privately. This Harry did, and an army car met him at the airport and took him to Mpolo at the Governor's Residence.

Harry had expected Mpolo's summons to do with the arrangements for his forthcoming official trip to Israel, but Mpolo immediately stated that this had been cancelled by Lumumba. The actual reason for his wish to see Harry was that Lumumba was about to change government policy in the Congo and move drastically to the left. This with the help of a *"certain embassy"* [undoubtedly the Soviet Embassy]. A reshuffle of the Government was secretly planned for 14 September, following which, those considered in opposition to Lumumba would be arrested. Although loyal to Lumumba, Mpolo told Harry that he couldn't let this happen for reasons of conscience. Therefore, he asked Harry to transmit this information to Kasavubu and, to show his good faith, passed Harry a list of those to be arrested. Amongst the nine names were those of Kasavubu and Mobutu.

When he returned to Leopoldville later that day, Harry- for undisclosed reasons- decided not to inform Avriel of this conversation.

The story goes on that Harry, using his special pass, managed to have a brief audience with Kasavubu, in which he handed over the list. The President promised to act, and asked Harry to keep the matter confidential. In turn Harry requested that protection be afforded to Mpolo, who had put the interests of the Republic above his personal loyalty to Lumumba. On 31 August 1960, Harry wrote to Kasavubu summarising their discussion. The original letter is reproduced on the following page.

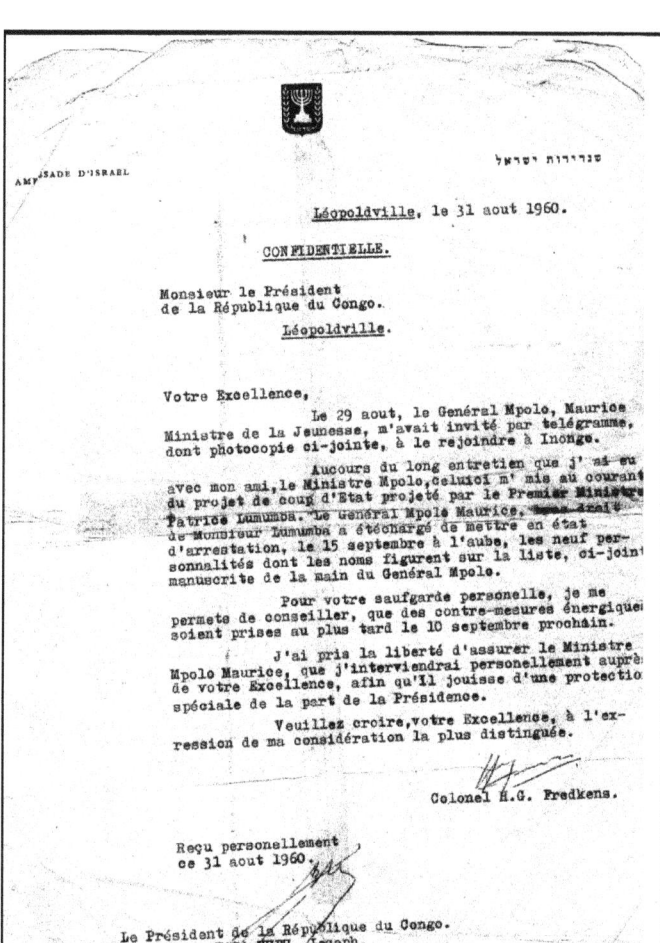

Letter Harry wrote to Kasavubu

This is a translation of the French text:

"To the President of the Republic of the Congo.

Leopoldville.

Your Excellency.
On 29 August General Maurice Mpolo, Youth Minister, invited me by telegram (copy attached), to join him in Inongo.
During the course of a long discussion which I held with my friend, Minister Mpolo, the latter informed me of a plan for a Coup d'état to be staged by the Prime Minister, Patrice Lumumba.
General Maurice Mpolo, the right hand of Mr. Lumumba, was given the task of arresting on 15 September at dawn, nine people whose names appear on the attached list, written in manuscript by General Mpolo.
For your personal safety, I respectfully advise that energetic counter measures be taken at the latest by 10 September next.
I have taken the liberty of reassuring Minister Maurice Mpolo that I would personally intervene with your Excellency, in order that he benefits from the special protection of the Presidency.

Yours Sincerely,
Colonel H.G.Fredkens

Personally acknowledged, this 31 August 1960

The president of the Republic of the Congo, Joseph KASA-WUBU"

On an attached handwritten list were the names of those Government officials to be arrested:

"Kasavubu Joseph, Kuna Emanuel, Mobutu Joseph, Monboko Justin, Moonsada Vital, Kuyena Esaie, Kiansa Nkongo, Thomas, Nkave Pascal, Bamba Emmanuel "

The historical record shows that Kasavubu did dismiss Lumumba on 5 September and in retaliation, Lumumba tried to remove Kasavubu. However, neither dismissal was approved by the members of Parliament and there was a stand-off. On 14 September Mobutu finally intervened, closed the parliament, arrested Lumumba and created a College of Commissioners, made up of university graduates, to run the country. He stated that his purpose was to allow a period of calm before restoring democratic rule once more.

At this point Harry was recalled to Israel .He later wrote that his involvement had become known to Lumumba's supporters and it was felt at the embassy that his life was in danger. Then, out of the blue, on 24 September 1960, he received a telegram in Israel with an invitation from Kasavubu to return to the Congo, as his economic advisor. On 30 October Harry wrote to the Director of the Foreign Office, Chaim Yahiel in the following terms:

"Dear Chaim Yahiel,

Further to our conversation regarding the telegraphic invitation received by me from Chief of State in Leopoldville, I am taking your advice to return there in continuation of the special mission I have been entrusted with in June 1960. This in order to give all assistance as needed to President Kasavubu.

Yours Faithfully,
Col. H.Fredkens"

This letter is significant in two ways. Firstly, it implied that Israel considered that Harry's particular skills served her policies well and secondly that, although employed by

President Kasavubu, Harry was, in reality, being seconded by the Foreign Ministry. It followed that Harry would consider that any actions he took in pursuance of his mission would be underwritten by the Ministry. This mistaken belief was to prove Harry's undoing, as later events were to show.

When Harry returned to the Congo in late October, still on his Israeli diplomatic passport, he tried in vain to discover the whereabouts of Mpolo. By the time Kasavubu re-established Parliament to its proper functions, Patrice Lumumba and his associates Maurice Mpolo and Joseph Okito had been taken to Katanga and executed. In his definitive book, published in 1999, entitled *"the Assassination of Lumumba"*, Ludo de Witte argued convincingly that Tshombe had arranged, on 17 January 1961, the execution of Lumumba, Mpolo and Okito with the help of Belgian officers serving in Katanga. However, there were also accomplices in Leopoldville and neither the UN nor the CIA escaped censure. At no time was there any official mention of Harry's or Israel's possible involvement. And yet in the 1980's when Harry was urgently pressing government ministers to provide him with financial support, he referred often to the work he carried out for the Israeli Government in respect of Lumumba. Here is a quote from a letter written by Harry on 16 October 1986. It was addressed:

"To whom it may concern:
After carrying out the highly illegal mission for the Israeli Foreign office, namely the Liquidation of the anti-Israeli Prime Minister Lumumba in Zaire, I returned to Israel for a short rest end of September 1960".

As Lumumba wasn't executed until January 1961, it must be assumed that Harry's use of the word" *liquidation*" doesn't signify" *assassination"* but rather, political marginalisation.

Kasavubu's authority in the Congo was largely circumscribed by the United Nations, which had placed its officials in key positions in the various ministries. They dominated the treasury, ensuring their almost complete control over national expenditure .Only provincial taxes and income from local purchase tax were under Congolese control. In these circumstances, Kasavubu looked to Harry to obtain economic assistance from abroad. However, despite his efforts he was not successful because of the unsettled situation in the Congo. A further problem was the lack of Congolese with managerial experience.

In January Harry crossed the Congo River to Congo–Brazzaville (former French Colony), where he had been invited to meet President Foulbert Youlou.

From there, on 23 January, Harry wrote in French to Ida to resolve a festering marital problem. He started his letter in terms of intense endearment, which were clearly designed to salvage a faltering marriage following a letter from Ida with accusations of infidelity.

"It is only you, you only, that I love. All momentary aberrations in my life caused by possibly irrational frustration, do not count for anything. There is only you, and there will always only be you. I cannot envisage being without you in my life..."

Further on in the letter he refers to the "*small intrigues of CHAMAT*" the company he had worked for in Dimona. These discreet allusions are a constant feature of Harry's letters to Ida and only the recipient would know what he meant. He referred to the possibility of working in the future as an engineer with Israel Libertovski, a well-known shipping magnate. There follows an impassioned statement which reflects Harry's innermost conviction:

"For twenty years I was my own boss. Whilst others, at this time of their life, can ease up, for me there is an uncertain and hard future. This doesn't frighten me, far from it, but all this had made me emotionally unbalanced. This is now in the past and, Pouskele, don't even think about it. This time I want to succeed in ensuring our future, so that we are independent in old age and not at the mercy of people who could fire me or discard me like an old pair of socks."

He told her that he would soon be leading a delegation of Congolese officials to Europe and then Israel. He mentions in passing that he was having difficulty in getting the Italians on board [To invest in the Congo] because of the Soviet influence in Central Africa. He reflected that the Hasson Brothers may be prepared to invest $1.5 million. In the meantime, he was engaged on a technical project which might net him, personally, about $20,000, which would enable them to invest in a "*Pardes*" which Ida had always wanted. [Investing in an apple or orange grove was a popular form of investment in Israel at the time.] Once this was achieved, he was prepared to work, either for Libertovski or for the "*Agence General*". He ended:

"Pouskele my little one, I regret all the upset that I have caused you. I love you and I have you under my skin, believe me."

It seems that with this letter Harry managed to retrieve the situation but this flaw in his character was not one easily remedied. Although not a particularly handsome man, Harry was adept at using his charm to good effect, particularly with beautiful women, whom he found irresistible. He once said to Ben that to attract women you had to make them laugh. This lowered their defences. The next thing was to feed them royally.

On 31 January, Fulbert Youlou wrote to President Ben Zvi of Israel with fulsome praise for Harry's qualities. He also stressed that Harry enjoyed his full confidence as well as that of President Kasavubu. He recommended that Ben Zvi:

"lend an attentive ear to Harry's knowledge of the problems of Central Africa which Harry wished to impart to him".

It would not be surprising if Harry had solicited this letter with a view to furthering his diplomatic career, if that were an option, after the end of his mission to the Congo.

The delegation, of which Harry was part, was to visit Europe for two months and then spend a few days in Israel. Its purpose was firstly to obtain arms supplies, despite the embargo imposed by the United Nations and then to learn about cooperative institutions in Israel. On 27 January, he received his official orders,from the Belgian military advisor to the ANC, Lieutenant Colonel Marliere, in the presence of General Joseph Mobutu and Justin Bomboko, the Foreign Minister. His task was to arrange the secret transport of arms from Europe to the port of Matadi in the Congo. The delegation was to be led by the Finance Minister Pascal Nkaye and included Senator Emmanuel Bamba.

At the beginning of March Harry was recalled from Europe to Leopoldville for six days in order to consult with President Kasavubu and President Youlou of Congo-Brazzaville. Their immediate concern was to procure a short-term loan equivalent to some 12 to 15 million Congolese Francs to be available by the end of March, at the latest, to charter boats to bring arms supplies from Europe. To avoid detection by the UN, it was proposed that the money, once received in Leopoldville, would be transferred with the connivance of the Brazzaville Government to their embassy in Paris. Kasavubu promised that the loan would be repaid one month later. Harry accepted the mission on the strict proviso that the loan would be made directly to the Congolese Defence Ministry.

It was then that Harry made a disastrous mistake. To procure the loan he approached former business acquaintances in the Congo, the Hasson Brothers. Asher and Leon Hasson were well respected businessmen in the Congo who had arrived from the Greek island of Rhodes in the late 1930s as part of a general exodus of the Jewish population. They ran one of the few clothes shops whose customers were both black and white. This unusual gesture was not forgotten by the new rulers after independence in 1960, and the Hasson Brothers continued to prosper in the Congo for many years.

From the Hassons' standpoint, the financial advantage of the proposed loan to the Defence Ministry was that the repayment would be made abroad thus enabling them to repatriate funds from the Congo, without the usual restrictions. The Hassons indicated that they could only advance 11.7 million Congolese Francs to the designated intermediary, Minister Isaie Kuyena, but to do this they would require an equivalent Dollar sum to be paid by way of guarantee. As Harry had access to funds in Switzerland, he arranged to meet Asher Hasson in Geneva to complete the transaction. There, on 14 March he handed over a Union de Banques Suisses Draft to Asher Hasson, in his name, for $210,000. The sum was debited by the bank to a company called Anderssen Registered Trust of which Harry was a director. At the same time Harry designed a formal receipt which he wanted signed by the President of the College of Commissioners, Justin Bomboko, on behalf of the Defence Ministry.

Harry later explained that he took on this temporary liability in view of the urgency of the matter, which did not allow him time to obtain the consent of the Israeli Foreign Ministry. Clearly with this lapse, he allowed himself to be financially exposed. He had placed complete reliance on the good faith of the Hasson Brothers and the Congolese Government. He was later to accuse both of embezzlement.

There is no dispute, however, that the money was effectively handed over to Kuyena, but,it never reached the Defence Ministry. A form of receipt, but not the one designed by Harry, was eventually produced some six months after the event. It read:

"Received from Colonel H.Fredkens the amount of 11 million seven hundred thousand Congolese francs by way of loan to the Defence Ministry of the Congolese Republic, transferred by wire to Paris for the needs of the Special Mission. This amount will be reimbursed in Paris at the end of 30 days."

It was signed by Kuyena. Later there was some controversy over why it bore two separate dates, 23 March and 21 April 1961.

Catastrophically for Harry, the loan was not repaid by the Congolese authorities either at the end of the designated one-month period nor at any time thereafter. Harry, eventually, had to reimburse the money himself. This particular saga will be covered in Chapter 7.

On the same day that Harry handed over the Bank Draft to Asher Hasson he wrote to Ida from the Hotel d'Angleterre, exhilarated that his own financial affairs were suddenly in good order. He had received a sum of $126,000 from the disposal of his business in the Congo, with a further $7,300 to come. It didn't compensate him for his overall losses in the Congo, but it would enable them to forget their worries and view the future with more confidence.

In assessing how he would invest the money, Harry earmarked about half to acquire a *"Pardes"* which could be rented out. Repairs to their house would be carried out and Harry would find an occupation to keep him busy, although he was not keen to invest in a business partnership. The possibility of working for Libertovski no longer interested him as much as finding a more suitable job in Tel Aviv. In view of their improved financial position, Harry recommended that Ida, who was working at the Duty Free shop in the Avia Hotel, cease her work. As for him, he had already visited Copenhagen, Rotterdam and Geneva and estimated that he would still be on the mission until the middle of May.

Whilst in Paris Harry received a letter from Vital Moanda dated 24 March. He was now head of the government of the Central Congo (which included the Bas-Congo), one of the states of the federation which it was now intended to create in the Republic. The impression given by the letter was that Harry was in fact working for this state and that he had *"carte blanche"* to act in its name in all matters concerning its economy and protection. He confirmed that Isaie Kuyena would temporarily be joining the delegation in Paris.

Now looking back, this letter has a certain significance because it is dated the day after Kuyena is alleged, according to the receipt he signed, to have received the money from Asher Hasson. We also now know that it was Moanda who gave the instruction to Kuyena to divert the funds away from the Ministry of Defence and into his Party's coffers. Could Moanda's exceptionally warm words towards Harry somehow have been linked to this unexpected windfall, but without revealing as much?

A few days later Kuyena arrived in Paris to join the delegation for its trip to Milan, Rome and Tel Aviv. Harry went ahead and met them in Tel Aviv on 28 March. During the delegation's stay until 6 April Harry introduced them to Levy Eshkol, Golda Meir and Chaim Yahil of the Foreign Ministry.

On 23 April Harry, back in Paris at the Hotel Martha, wrote to Ida that he regretted that he would not be finished until June or July. He mentioned in passing the ongoing OAS scare, when a parachutist putsch from Algeria was anticipated by the French President, General de Gaulle. In the meantime, he told Ida that he missed her terribly. Again, he insisted that she soon gave notice to end her contract at the Avira Hotel. He was now disinclined to return to Africa and intended to return to Israel at the end of July. Harry mentioned a possible job opportunity for him there as the technical representative of a French Company. If that came off, he would have to attend a short technical course. Clearly Harry's attention was not exclusively devoted to his mission but to business or job opportunities which he could exploit once it had come to an end. As always, Harry was looking for the chance to ensure their financial stability. In his usual manner, Harry ended his letter with endearments to Ida, asking her to give *a "Kwetch"* [Yiddish for a squeeze] to Annette.

Some indication of the Congolese delegation's work on arms procurement is indirectly provided in British archival documentation. These indicate attempts to ship arms to Congo (Brazzaville), the ex-French colony, whose president Fulbert Youlou was a close friend of Kasavubu. Given that his forces only comprised some fully armed 120 soldiers and 600 Gendarmes, it seemed inconceivable to the British Embassy that there was a requirement for such large arms shipments. The logical answer was that the arms were really destined for Leopoldville on the other side of the Congo River. Here are a few examples of these transactions: (a) On 6 March the British Secretary for the Colonies was informed from Malta that an aircraft had landed from Milan bearing 93 boxes marked *"Berretta arms"*. The plane's manifest indicated that the arms were destined for Brazzaville. (b) On 18 May the British Embassy in Brazzaville reported to the Foreign Office that a Mr. Menachem Arazi had been instrumental in placing an order for arms with a British firm, A.H.Mitchell (Firearms) Ltd. for export to Congo (Brazzaville).[18]

This order apparently upset the French government as President Youlou was bound by agreement to make all his arms purchases from France or by approval of the French authorities. In the event the Board of Trade refused an export licence. (c) In August the British Board of Trade informed the Foreign Office about an application from a company called Sidem (U.K) Ltd for a transhipment licence for a large supply of arms which they wished to export to Brazzaville. The arms were to be shipped from Haifa, Israel to Pointe Noire in the Congo, via the United Kingdom. When the Board attempted to contact Sidem at their address in Dover Street, London they were told they had moved. The Board concluded that this was only an accommodation address and refused the transhipment licence. In addition to the order on Mitchell, the Board had previously refused an export licence to I.C.I to ship two million 7.62 cartridges to Brazzaville. Interestingly, the order for these cartridges had been placed with I.C.I. by Sidem International Company of Brussels.[19] The particular attempt to tranship Israeli arms to the Congo via the UK (presumably on a British ship) was obviously a ploy to disguise their origin from prying UN eyes. In view of Harry's history of attempting to circumvent British bureaucracy, it is not mere speculation to discern his hand in all these transactions.

From May to August Harry divided his time between Geneva, Paris, Brussels, Milan and Rome. In his letters he complained about the inefficiency of the Congolese and that his health was not good. He no longer had the energy required for the mission.

In May, whilst he was in Paris, Harry went on a large-scale shopping expedition on behalf of Ida and Annette,

---

[18] . N.A FO 371/155141
[19] N.A FO 371/155141

for high quality clothing which was not available in Israel at that time. He knew their sizes perfectly and had no qualms about buying the more intimate of garments. He then went on to buy them beauty products. He had immaculate taste and cost was no object. It appears that Harry's financial situation seemed relatively secure as he wrote to Ida on 13 May that:

"I have achieved the objective I set myself and I don't have to be a rich man. I have enough put by for our needs. I only need to have a few jobs which interest me. My security I have in my nice little family and six dogs. What more do I need?. I have bought myself two hunting rifles and would like to buy a Springer Cockle Spaniel, trained for hunting like Nicky in the Congo. We will call him Taboo and, in this way, Nicky will have a companion. Don't forget to send me the estimate for the house repairs and check with Macky , the lawyer to see how the "pardes" project is advancing. When you come here we will buy garden furniture, crockery, a fridge, a bridge table. We will take all this back on the boat as well as the car and the dog."

Eleven days later Harry wrote from Brussels to say that he had been to England for 5 days and had visited his cousin Ralph in Blackpool. He was surprised to learn from Ralph's wife Sissy, that Ida had informed her that she had no intention of giving up her job, when he finally returned to Tel Aviv. He indicated that he had encountered some political difficulties in his work and that he had come to Brussels to deal with them. In passing, he mentioned that he was writing a book called *"I chose Falafel"*. Presumably intended as a humorous reflection on his decision to settle in Israel. Like the Arazi manuscript, this book too, did not see the light of day.

In mid-June, at Harry's request, Justin Bomboko, the Congolese Foreign Minister wrote to Andre Spaak, his opposite number in Belgium, about arrangements for the transport of merchandise purchased by the Congolese delegation in various European countries. He confirmed that Harry was acting on behalf of the government and that he would appreciate all assistance being given to him to facilitate his endeavours. He guaranteed that Harry would exercise the maximum of discretion in dealing with this matter. After the initial fiasco, Harry had found a way, with Belgian help, to expedite the arms purchases to the Congo. An example of the benevolent attitude of the Belgians towards Harry is a commendation he received in June 1981, no doubt solicited by him, from *the "Belgian Association of Interests in Africa"*. It recognises the aid given to Belgian interests and Belgians in the Congo, as a result of his efforts, during the early days of independence. Particularly it confirms that in respect of Lumumba *"Sworn enemy of Belgium and the Belgians"* that Harry was instrumental in his dismissal and arrest.

At the end of June Harry was joined by Ida for a holiday which took in Paris, the French Midi, Switzerland, Spain and England over a 6-week period. She had not left Israel since her return from the Congo in 1959. As Harry was still retained on business in Europe, she returned alone by boat to Haifa with all their purchases, the car and the dog.

On 20 December 1961 Harry wrote to Justin Bomboko from Rome, confirming a meeting that he had held with him and General Mobutu. He enclosed Kuyena's receipt for the 11.7 million Congolese Francs in respect of the temporary loan to the Ministry of Defence, made through the intermediary of the Hasson Brothers. However, as the sum had not been repaid, he had asked the Anderssen Company of Geneva to debit the Congolese Government with the equivalent dollar value of $210,000. Many years later Harry stated that:

"for very valid political reasons , Messrs. Anderssen abstained from applying for the settlement of any outstanding accounts until 1971"

In effect, it was only the severance of Israeli diplomatic ties with the Congo that led Harry to get in touch with the Zairean authorities to press for payment.

According to Harry, the mission having come to an end in August 1961 he relinquished his post with Kasavubu at the end of the year. A factor contributing to this decision was the mysterious disappearance of four of his Congolese friends and his awareness of ongoing intrigues by Bomboko and Mobutu to eventually replace Kasavubu. This knowledge Harry imparted to Kasavubu before he left the Congo, this time for good.

On 24 November 1965, Mobutu staged a bloodless coup and became President of the country, later to be renamed Zaire

Joseph Kasavubu, President, Patrice Lumumba, Prime Minister and Baudouin, King of the Belgians

Congo Independence celebrations 30 June 1960

Harry (on right) with Israeli delegation. Presentation of credentials by Ehud Avriel to President Kasavubu

In foreground: Patrice Lumumba, Maurice Mpolo and Joseph Okito

In January 1961 all 3 ministers were executed by firing squad in Katanga

Harry with President Kasavubu on left and Isaie Kuyena on right. (after recall to the Congo to the post of economic Advisor to the President (October 1960)

Chapter 7 Harry's third family 1961-1971

[Break up of his second marriage followed by a new relationship. In addition, we observe how his lack of financial caution finally catches up with him with disastrous consequences.]

In the early part of 1962 Harry spent time between Geneva and Paris. This marked Harry's venture into the arms trade, a vocation for which, in view of his previous experiences, he was admirably suited. The vehicle for his transactions was the Anderssen Registered Trust Company in Geneva. He also set up a subsidiary company, Anderssen (Israel) Ltd. in Israel. He also traded as A&A Anderssen. Harry acted as the middleman between Government arms supply agencies in Europe and the eventual customers. To act as an official arms dealer Harry had always to acquire an *"End User Certificate"* from the Government to whom the arms shipments were destined and present this to the supplying Government agency. However, it was not difficult to procure an *End User Certificate* from a corrupt Government official of SAY: a South American country. The eventual customer for the arms was therefore not necessarily a sovereign Government and Harry was therefore implicated in what one could characterise as some *"shady deals"* with dissident forces. Ben often warned him about the risks he was running in the arms business. At one stage in 1974 Harry entrusted to *"Mac"*, Ben's friend in Brussels, an envelope of documents to be handed over to the authorities should some mishap befall him, during one of his journeys." *Mac"* confirmed to me that, much later, on Harry's instructions, he destroyed the contents of the envelope. Certainly, no documents ever came into my possession which would confirm the details of transactions which Harry had been involved in during this period in his career. However, according to Ben, arms such as the Swiss Oerlikon anti-aircraft gun, the Belgium Vigneron sub-machine gun and the British Sten gun were all part of Harry's arms inventory. Ben recalled twice visiting Brescia to collect expensive gifts on Harry's behalf from the Berretta arms manufacturer. By 1965 Harry was no longer active in the arms trade, possibly because, according to Ben, of pressure from the Israeli authorities, who themselves were heavily engaged in this area.

In April 1962 Harry wrote to Ida from Geneva confirming that he had raised funds to buy Annette a flat as a wedding present. At the same time, he had also sent a formal demand to the Congolese Authorities for the repayment of the loan to his Anderssen Company. He received no response and let the matter lie.

In October 1962 Annette was married to Mordechai Duenias in the family home at 16 Rechov Hazait. Harry appears in the wedding photograph looking somewhat portly and ageing. After his long absence from Israel, Harry settled down to a somewhat tenuous life with Ida. Their circle of friends tended to be the English-speaking residents of the *"Schechounot"*, many of whom had been in the IAF. To one of them, Yehoshua Gilutz, Harry brought a dog from Europe and sold him his Jaguar. From the time that he first met him in the RAF in Cairo in 1945, Yehoshua appreciated Harry for his sense of humour and ability to tell a good story, many of which he thought exaggerated. There was no doubt that at social gatherings his charisma was very evident, but it was Ida's good looks and attractive personality that charmed their friends. In this period of Harry's life, money did not seem to be a problem. In June 1963, Harry wrote to Ben whilst he was in Rio de Janeiro, Brazil and told him that he would send him a return air ticket to come to Israel with a return to Brussels after a month. Whilst regretting that Ben's wife at the time, Edith, could not come to Israel as well, he promised to visit her in Brussels, whilst he was there for a fortnight at the end of July. He even promised to give her a cheque to cover her *"outings to cabarets"*, whilst Ben was in Israel. In an intriguing aside, Harry indicated that he would join Ben for two to three months in Brazil the following year. Whilst there, he was thinking of doing a film on the Amazon with the French Filmex Company, in which he had *"some interests"*. Obviously, Harry's search for new business ventures knew no bounds, even if they were often pipe dreams.

Harry soon became partners with a gentleman called Lahav in a shirt-making factory. To promote the export sales, he had again to travel abroad, which suited Harry's restless personality and love of Europe. There, Yehoshua said, Harry made a *"Booboo"*. Instead of selling shirts he was making time with a young woman and enjoying the high life. This information got back to Ida, but this time she was in less of a forgiving mood. They had reached the lowest point in their marriage and they decided to part amicably. Ida retained her friends in their social circle, but Harry found himself excluded. A divorce was eventually granted by the rabbinate in May 1964. Surprisingly, Harry continued to live in Schechounot Hakatzinim until January 1965, when Ida asked him to leave. He then departed for Europe to follow his business career but continued to write to Ida expressing his terrible loneliness at being separated from her. All the while he expressed his hope that, somehow, they would be reconciled. He recognised, nevertheless the pain he had caused her and promised to meet his commitment to pay maintenance money, although he was in financial difficulty. These latter sentiments are expressed in the last of 24 letters that Harry wrote to Ida from January 1961 to October 1965, which were retained by Annette after her mother's death.

In August 1963, Harry visited Malmo and met Lilian Gennser. She was his father's great niece and, at the time, was 30 years old. She was in the fashion trade and articles about her appeared in the local press together with some of the dress designs. As she relates, with impish humour, compared to now she was then something of a beauty. Today she lives quietly in retirement with her dog and cat in a small village, a few kilometres north of Tel Aviv. Her daughter and her family live close by.

Harry visited Lilian's home to see her elderly mother, who was his cousin, It was a difficult period in Lilian's life as she had recently lost her fiancé to cancer after a year's struggle. She had also lost her father when she was only 8 years old and possibly Harry helped to fill this double void in her life. She found him very understanding, charming and particularly humorous. To lift her spirits, he regaled her with naughty jokes. She remembered his well–kept manicured fingers and his overall smart appearance. He told her that he was in the process of divorce and was quite frank about his past infidelities. He then invited her to London for a week-end trip and, despite her mother's misgivings, she accepted the offer. Clearly, she became infatuated with him. A few weeks later, after he had left Sweden, she phoned him to tell him that she was pregnant. He quickly responded that they would eventually marry and settle in Israel. As it happened, she suffered a miscarriage, but this did not affect their plans. She was keen to start a new life, away from the influence of her brother and sister who tended to treat her as the kid sister. Had Harry not been so young in spirit and anxious to please her, their difference in age (he was then 58 years old) might have been a problem. Certainly, her mother had thought so, but this did not deter her.

It was only in 1965 that Harry was ready to marry Lilian. But in Malmo they could only have a civil marriage as the Synagogue's Rabbi was away on holiday. The next day, however, they were able to have a religious marriage in Copenhagen. Harry then had to go away again on business and for two months she travelled around with him, visiting Belgium, France and Italy. Whilst there he became ill, suffering from a recurrence of a cerebral spasm, which arose from his air crash years previously. This produced a slight paralysis in his right arm and balance problems, from which he soon recovered. Later in Sweden and Paris he bought furniture for their future home which he was going to build on a plot he had acquired in Caesarea. Before he went away again, he bought Lilian a Saab station wagon as a wedding present.

About this time, whilst still abroad, he went into property development in Israel with a gentleman called Teperson, but for Harry this proved to be a bad venture and he was not able to profit from his investment. The shirt business eventually failed, and he was owed money by Lahav.

On 15 September 1965, Harry brought his second Jaguar back to Israel and he settled in a flat Ida found for him in Ramat Gan. Only then did Harry accept that he had reached the point of no return with Ida.[20]

At this point, Harry invited Lilian to come over from Malmo to join him. So, in late October she drove down in her Saab through Germany to Marseilles to take the boat for Israel. As she got ready to get off the boat in Haifa, she heard her name being called over the boat's loudspeaker *"Mrs.Lilian Fredkens come to the purser's office"*. She was told that Harry had arranged to speed her through the disembarkation formalities and soon she and Harry were on their way to Tel Aviv. On the way south they stopped in Caesarea to see how work was proceeding on their plot, but it took a year before they were able to move from Ramat Gan. In the meantime, Harry tried to get Lilian to go to an Ulpan to learn Hebrew but without

---

[20] Ida died in November 1981 at the age of 62

success. For himself, he was most at home speaking English.

Picking up domestic life in Israel, Lilian's visits to the local *"Makolet"* (grocery shop) were particularly fraught as she was appalled at the behaviour of the customers, especially the unhygienic way they handled foodstuffs. She readily admitted that she avoided confrontation in general and being Swedish born had great difficulty with Israeli culture which seemed to thrive on it. She recognised that as she couldn't bridge the cultural gap that separated her from the local population, she would just make the best of it. Not so Harry, whose level of tolerance was virtually non-existent and who expressed his disapproval in whatever Hebrew words he could muster on the occasion. This must have been very frustrating for a man who, in other languages such as French and English, was so articulate.

Lilian then recalls the advent of the Six-Day War in June 1967, when she refused her mother's request that she return to Sweden. Harry became the daily source of information and analysis on the war for their few neighbours in Caesarea. From his own war experience and knowledge of the IDF and the IAF he predicted accurately what was likely to happen. In the same period, whilst Lilian was pregnant with Micky, they went to a concert and in the crowd was Ida. Harry pointed her out but made no move to introduce Lilian to her. In September Micky was born.

Years later they saw Ida sitting in a café with friends. But Harry again failed to make the introductions, yet he did take Micky over to show him off to Ida. This reluctance on the part of Harry to introduce a former wife to Lilian did not extend to his first wife Rosette (Zus) when she visited Israel on Wizo business in the early 1970s. She stayed at Caesarea and Harry was highly amused that she and Lilian got on so well together. This had also been the case in the Congo, when Rosette first met Ida in 1946. It is interesting to speculate whether all three present and former wives might have equally enjoyed each other's company, had Harry dared to try and arrange such a reunion. Before Harry and Lilian moved to Caesarea, they used to visit Annette and Mordechai regularly on a Friday night. However, Lilian never understood why Harry avoided introducing her to Ida.

My own belief is that Ida had been such an extremely precious part of Harry's life, that the pain of their parting was a constant reminder of what he had so foolishly lost. The only way for him to deal with this burden and his feelings of guilt was to suppress that part of his life from his memory and pretend she had not existed. Thus, once he was married to Lilian and had children with her, he lied to new acquaintances, stating that he had only been married once before and had a son from that marriage.

After the failure of his previous business ventures he and Lilian opened an art gallery in the old minaret of Caesarea. After the first successful year, the advent of competition in the area, made it far less profitable and they closed it. The remaining paintings Harry tried to sell in Belgium with Ben's help but without much success. After that Harry, with his technical skills, designed and produced, in a small factory, wrought iron artefacts, such as lamps, which were then allied with a glass blowing venture. But Harry, being Harry, soon got bored with that too. Lilian learnt to deal with his temperament by ignoring the occasional outbursts, when he became frustrated. He laughingly complained that she was so even-tempered that he couldn't even have a proper row with her.

In 1971, financial calamity struck when Harry was suddenly forced to repay the 1961 loan, which had remained dormant for so long that he had practically forgotten about it. At least that was how he explained it to Lilian. She stood by Harry as, in June 1972, they sold their beautiful villa in Caesarea. When that was not enough to cover the debt, she sold her jewellery as well and apparently family members abroad also contributed. They moved to Pardes Hannah where, on 1 August their daughter, Mina, was born. Increasing financial constraints forced the whole family to move the following September to a small flat in Netanya. In all, they made two subsequent moves in Netanya. Family life, despite their obvious financial difficulties, revolved around their young children.

At home the children spoke Swedish with Lilian and with Harry they spoke English. Later at school they both spoke Hebrew. Harry used to play a lot with the children. Micky did not realise that Harry was a particularly old father (he was then about 68), until one day, when he was about 6, a friend of his referred to Harry as his grandfather. This upset him and it took all of Lilian's persuasive power to convince him that he lost nothing from having an elderly father, given the time that *"Pappy"* was able to spend with him, unlike other boys' fathers.

About this time Harry's health began to deteriorate. He had previously suffered from cerebral spasms and loss of balance and this became more pronounced. His anxieties about his financial problems and the need to provide for his young family exacerbated the problem. By now he was no longer working, and Lilian took up a job at the Netanya Diamond Centre showing busloads of visitors around and explaining the various processes. As to Harry, he launched a crusade to recover the $210,000 that he had lost.

In 1972 Harry was adjudicated bankrupt and could no longer involve himself in business ventures. To all intents and purposes, he was retired. At their home in Netanya, to help balance the very restricted family budget, he assisted Lilian in making dolls and toys, which she sold to local shops. In her younger years she had been a fashion designer and now these latent skills, in view of their state of penury, became very useful.

In 1976, taking a temporary break, he sat down at his much –abused typewriter and began to write the tale of

Yehuda Arazi, hoping that its publication would help the family's fortunes. But fate, as usual, decided otherwise and publication never took place.

Ben and Edith's wedding in 1957. Rosette, Ben's mother is seated to the left of the bride and Annette is seated on the floor in front of the bride.

Harry and Ben eating out in Brussels during one of their infrequent meetings. (Circa 1961)

Annette's Wedding to Mordechai Duenias in 1962. Harry and Ida are on the left

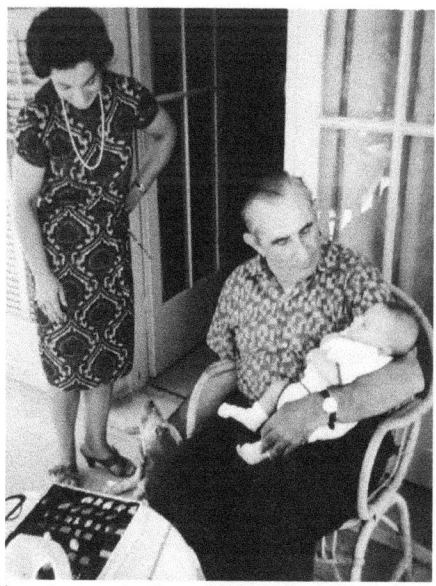

Harry holding Annette's first child, Schmulik, in 1964. Ida is on the left

David Ben Gurion as the guest of honour at a reception given by Harry's company: A & A Anderssen.(Circa 1969) Harry is seated next to Pinhas Sapir the Minister of Finance.

Chapter 8: The Fight for Justice 1971-1989

[This is perhaps the most humiliating chapter in Harry's life. A Wide-ranging exchange of correspondence provided by Lilian, often with allusions to fraud and intrigue by State and other actors, is explored in depth. Ultimately, it is a story of increasing disillusionment and the desperation of a man, in severe financial difficulties and increasing ill health, anxious to restore the fortunes of his young family, whilst he was still alive]

From 1972 on, Harry's aim was to recover from any source he felt liable, morally or legally, his lost fortune.

As time passed, Harry became increasingly convinced that the Israeli establishment and especially the Foreign Ministry deliberately placed obstacles in his way for reasons of national policy. In practice this meant avoiding any action which could seriously affect diplomatic relations between Israel and Zaire under Joseph Mobutu.

The basic facts about the $210,000 loan made in March 1961 have already been covered in Chapter 6. It will be recalled that the only apparent proof that the Congolese authorities had received the equivalence in Congo francs of the cheque paid to Asher Hasson was a form of receipt on a scrappy piece of paper, signed by Isaie Kuyena, which had been forwarded to Harry in September 1961.

In Harry's view, if the receipt was a forgery or had been obtained from Kuyena in an underhand way, then the Hassons were guilty of embezzlement. On the other hand, if the receipt was genuine, then the current Congolese Government had to accept liability as Kuyena, a Government Minister, had diverted the funds.

Harry's first step, in December 1971, was to write to the Congolese Ambassador in Jerusalem setting out the basis of his claim. On 26 June 1972, while still at Pardes

Hannah, he had a meeting with the Ambassador and subsequently furnished him with greater details of the Hasson Brothers involvement. In the same month, using a twin-track approach, he had written to Asher Hasson in Belgium, enclosing copies of the relative documents in his possession, demanding redress for the financial loss he had suffered plus accumulated interest. This claim was formulated on the basis that in 1961 the Hasson Brothers had not followed his instructions to ensure that the money had reached the proper recipient. Asher Hasson was surprised and outraged by this demand as he had had various meetings with Harry since 1961 and the subject of such a claim had never been raised. He was particularly worried that Harry's attempt to involve the current Government of Zaire in this affair, could put the interests of the Hasson Brothers at risk as well as their lives. To counteract this danger, Asher Hasson contacted the Israeli Ambassador in Belgium, Moshe Alon, arguing that Harry's various activities were also endangering the existence of the Jewish Community in Zaire and Israel's relations with that country. Alon was sufficiently disturbed by this news to write to Mordecai Shalev, head of the African desk at the Israeli Foreign Office on 6 July. He enclosed the various documents that Harry had sent to Hasson. Unfortunately for Alon, as a later court case was to reveal, he was very indiscreet in his condemnations of Harry, attacking his credibility in business affairs and characterising Harry's letter to Hasson as being threatening. He also intimated that Harry, forgetting the good things that the Hassons had done for him in the Congo, was now attempting to benefit from their apparent wealth. Taking a partisan approach, he had nothing but praise for the Hasson family and their devotion to Israel.

Shalev's response was to involve Ehud Avriel, Harry's old boss. They both had a meeting with Harry at which they admonished him for his contacts with the Zairian Embassy. They attempted to persuade him that, for the sake of the Jewish Community in Zaire and Israel's relations with that country, he should avoid court proceedings and instead accept arbitration over the issue.

Shalev proposed to Avriel that Michael Tsur, the Director General of the Ministry of Commerce, should be the arbitrator, Avriel then sent a letter to Tsur on 17 July suggesting, that, in view of Harry's *"state of total despair after another bankruptcy"*, Hasson should give Harry $20,000 in full settlement. He also enclosed a copy of Harry's letter to Hasson. On 23 July Shalev sent the documents he had received from Alon, together with Alon's covering letter, to Michael Tsur. He expressed the hope that *"you will help to liquidate this saga in a peaceful way"*. All this correspondence remained unknown to Harry until well after the arbitration. For him, it clearly represented a concerted move by members of the Israeli Foreign Office to influence the arbitrator's eventual decision.

On 11 October Harry responded to a letter from Michael Tsur. He acknowledged that should he and Asher Hasson fail to resolve the matter during the latter's visit to Israel, then both parties would agree to his appointment as sole arbitrator and that his decision would be binding.

Harry duly met Asher and Leon Hasson on 19 November. That night he wrote a note to Tsur summarising the admissions he had elicited from the Hassons. Firstly, that when they accepted to advance 11.7million Congolese Francs to the Congolese Government they were entirely without funds and had to extend bills of exchange to meet the commitment. Secondly, that they had immediately cashed the $210,000 cheque in Brussels and received the equivalence in Congolese francs on the black market in Leopoldville at well above the official rate, netting them a substantial profit. As to the famous *"Receipt"* with its two dates, the Hassons stated that the payment to Kuyena had been made in two instalments. This Harry refused to accept, especially as Kuyena on 28 March 1961 had said to him in Israel that he had not seen the Hasson Brothers for quite some time and had not received anything from them. He therefore contended to Tsur that the receipt had been obtained from Kuyena at a later date through bribery. Furthermore, he contended that the Hassons had convinced Kuyena that, because it was an illegal transaction, he should not fear exposure. Harry's subsequent letters to Kuyena, suggesting that he had received the money and used it for other purposes than what was intended, remained without reply. Harry had always felt sure that the Congolese Government had received the money. Now he wasn't that sure!

At the end of the meeting the Hasson Brothers stated there was nothing to agree with Harry and proposed moving to arbitration.

The arbitration took place on 20 November 1972 in the office of Michael Tsur with both parties present. After a few hours Michael Tsur dismissed Harry's claim and rendered a verdict in favour of Asher Hasson. This was confirmed in January 1973. But, quite extraordinarily, Tsur then convinced Hasson that in view of Harry's precarious financial situation he should agree to making an ex gratia lump sum payment of $3,000 and thereafter monthly payments of $150 per month for the rest of Harry's life. In a letter to Tsur on 26 December Harry agreed that this arrangement, once implemented, would prevent any further claims against the Hasson Brothers. The payments were put into effect but were then stopped in June 1973 when Harry attempted to bring charges against the Hasson Brothers in the Belgian courts. In July 1973 Harry attempted to coerce Michael Tsur into reversing his arbitration decision. He threatened that his lawyer in Belgium would hand over to the Zairian Authorities documents referring to the complicity of the Hasson Brothers in the affair. However, if his requirements were met, he would take steps to protect the

Hassons from harassment in Kinshasa (Ex-Leopoldville). A meeting with Tsur in August, in which he tried to convince Harry that, whatever he did, he wouldn't receive a penny from the Zairian authorities, failed to impress Harry, who threatened to subpoena him in a future court action.

The records show that in 1974 Michael Tsur was forced to resign his position in Government and was indicted for fraud, bribery and breach of trust whilst he was in his post. An article in Yediot Ahronot in May 1974 briefly detailed the story of the $210,000 loan. It indicated that Harry was seeking an annulment of the arbitration decision on the grounds that Michael Tsur had not been an objective arbitrator.

During Tsur's trial in 1975, at the end of which he was convicted and sentenced to 15 years imprisonment, various documents came to light which involved the 1972 arbitration. In Harry's view these showed that certain members of the Foreign Office had exercised undue influence on the process. He therefore approached the Attorney General to investigate his allegation. This was rejected and Harry therefore applied to the Tel Aviv District Court to have the arbitration decision annulled. The story was now in the public domain. Inevitably the claims, by a former Colonel in the Israeli Air Force, of judicial wrongdoing aroused the interest of the press.

In July 1975, a detailed article appeared in Ma'ariv. In this Harry claimed that several documents had come to light since Tsur's arrest which pointed to inappropriate behaviour by three officials at the Foreign Ministry. The documents referred to were the July 1972 correspondence between Moshe Alon, Mordecai Shalev and Ehud Avriel, although they were not specifically named in the article.

Following a request for clarification, the Foreign Office spokesman, Schmuel Moyal, accused Harry of attempting to embarrass the foreign Office and certain staff members. However, a court official conceded that, whilst everybody had acted in good faith, possibly some legal damage had been done by relaying the confidential letters to Tsur. He added that, in retrospect, Tsur should have disqualified himself from the arbitration. This conciliatory tone was then spoiled by his next remark:

"The Foreign Ministry did a lot for Fredkens and this is the wrong way to thank us."

Harry's reported response was true to form:

"I did a lot for this country and I don't ask for a reward but at least they should not put a knife in my back!"

The issue of the arbitration was finally settled in April 1976, when Judge Harish of the Tel Aviv District Court found in favour of Harry and annulled the arbitration decision. He stated:

"It is heart-breaking to see the elite of the Foreign Office, people with a reputation, stoop to deal in this way in a matter of Justice".

Whilst Harry had been busy preparing his case in Israel, he had not neglected his pursuit of the Zairian authorities. In April 1973 the Zairian General Auditor of the Armed Forces wrote to the Hasson Brothers asking for confirmation of the payment of 11.7 million Congolese francs to the ex-Government Minister Kuyena on behalf of the Congolese Government. As the Hasson Brothers made no response to this letter, Harry wrote to the Zairian Ambassador in Jerusalem setting out in detail the answers to the questions posed. He also stated that, graphology had established beyond doubt, the signatures on the receipt had indeed been those of Kuyena. Again, he related the details of the mission he had been sent on in January 1961 by Bomboko and Mobutu. He now demanded that either he receive full reimbursement plus interest or conversely, confirmation from the General Auditor that Kuyena had not received the money and that the receipt was a forgery. He stated that, if he did not receive within a month a favourable reply, he would take action to protect his interests. Clearly no reply was forthcoming. Harry's lawyers in Belgium wrote themselves to the General Auditor in January 1974. They indicated that they had sent some 15 letters in the space of a year to the Zairian Ministry of Defence and the Zairian Ambassador in Belgium only to learn that the dossier was still under review. At this point the correspondence with the Zairian authorities seems to have come to a stop, possibly because Harry was now involved in the court proceedings in Israel. In any event any hope of recovering the money from Zaire seems to have been delusional given the nature of Mobutu's regime.

This was a regime which systematically robbed its people of their share of the vast mineral wealth of the Congo. Only Mobutu's immediate entourage benefited from the vast funds arriving in the country and from Western political support. Mobutu was profligate in acquiring innumerable properties across Europe. Seven hundred miles from the capital he created his own *"Versailles in the Country"* enclave, with musical fountains, ornamental lakes, private zoos, golden pagodas and a palace covering 15,000 square meters with Italian marble, French antiques and Venetian glassware. The debt owed to Harry paled into insignificance against such manifestations of obscene wealth and Mobutu could easily have settled it, should he have felt so inclined.

The next document, made available by Lilian, is dated July 1979. In view of the lapse of time it is probable that other pertinent letters went astray over the years. This letter was addressed to Meir Aranne, the Legal Advisor to the Prime Minister's Office. As usual with Harry's correspondence it was written in English. It refers in the main to Judge Harish's judgement but also contains three significant assertions by Harry:

Firstly, he refers to a mission:

"duly carried out on orders of the Israeli Foreign Office and culminating with the liquidation of Prime Minister Patrice Lumumba."

and secondly that:

"this was but one mission carried out for the State for ONE DOLLAR per year and in the course of which I more than once stuck out my neck."

His next assertion, however, is undoubtedly libellous, but in character:

"My lawyer is ready at any moment to produce full evidence of the important embezzlement by the Hasson brothers of Brussels and the frantic and criminal protection given by the trio of charlatans of the Israeli Foreign Office."

Obviously, he was referring, none too diplomatically, to Shalev, Alon and Avriel.

During the 1970's and early 1980s Harry frequently visited Belgium to prepare a court case against the Hasson Brothers. In 1975 he became very friendly with Ben's friend, *"Mac"*, (Mark Felix) who was an avid African art collector. Whilst Harry was staying in Ben's house during his absence abroad, the two of them would get together once or twice a week. Despite their wide difference in age they struck up a good rapport and *"Mac"* was an avid listener of Harry's tales of the Congo, the war and Israel. However, he soon recognised Harry's obsession with the loan affair and the Hasson Brothers and tried to dissuade him from throwing good money after bad in hopeless litigation processes. He, like Ben, did not succeed. At one time Harry sought to inveigle him and Ben into a business transaction with doubtful overtones. It involved a trip to Koningsburg in Poland to retrieve a genuine painting by Durer, in the possession of a private individual in need of western money. As Ben's second wife, Anita, spoke Polish, she was delegated with *"Mac"* and a Belgian art expert to visit Poland. *"Mac"* was to pretend to the Polish Communist authorities that he wanted to paint Polish landscapes and would need to take his equipment with him. The idea was to hide the Durer among a few paintings that *"Mac"* produced and so smuggle it over the frontier. As it happens, the Durer turned out to be a 19th century fake and not worth the millions that Harry had suggested they would all make out of the venture. After Harry came out with some other implausible money-making ideas, they had to tell him that they were no longer interested.

"Mac" also mentioned that once when he visited Harry at Ben's house, he found him in the company of several Congolese businessmen and politicians. They were all having a good time together and were obviously old friends of Harry's. As to whether the meeting was more than just social," *Mac"* was unable to say. Given that Harry was meeting Congolese at the height of his vigorous campaign to recover his funds from their authorities, this social activity appears to be somewhat inexplicable.

Harry's lonely fight for justice, received a welcome boost from an unexpected source in 1980. A former IAF fighter pilot by the name of Eli Eyal contacted him one day and asked to come and see him in Netanya. Eli, as a reserve lieutenant Colonel in the IAF, had been working in the Historical Division and came across Harry's exploits in various documents. Although Eli, had been a pilot in the famous 101 Squadron in the Negev in 1948, he had not come across Harry. In later life, when he was about 57, he became keen to seek him out. When he met Harry he was appalled at the conditions he was living under. He was even more outraged when Harry explained his long crusade both with the Congolese and the Israeli foreign Ministry to recover his lost fortune. Harry gave him a copy of his manuscript on Yehuda Arazi's trip to Italy, which he was trying to publish in the USA, as no Israeli publishing house was interested.

Eli, determined to help Harry in any way he could, set about involving former IAF colleagues to bring pressure to bear on the powers that be and especially the Foreign Ministry. His contacts included Ezer Weizman, Aharon Remez and Dan Tolkovski, all previous commanders of the IAF and Alex Zieloni, the former Chief of Staff of Sherut Ha'Avir. All, to some degree, brought their influence to bear, but their only success, sometime later, was with the Ministry of Defence under Yitzhak Rabin.

During a protracted campaign, Harry had tried to resolve his claim against the IDF for an adequate pension. At the time he only had a 32% disability pension which arose from his plane crash in 1948. He took up with the Ministry of Defence, then under Ariel Sharon, their refusal, on technical grounds, to award him a pension related to services to the State before it was created and his subsequent three-year service in the IAF. In a letter dated 15 November 1982, prepared for Harry in Hebrew, he expressed his innermost feelings about the way he had been treated. This is a full English translation:

"To the Minister of Defence, 15 November 1982
Subject: My service in the army 1948-1951.
This letter is written after a conversation with Mr. Weizman.

Many years ago my lawyer Mr. Von Weizel submitted to your office the details of my service for Israel's security long before the State was born and made a request for me to receive a pension. At the time your office stopped handling my case saying there was some mistake about the dates of my service. Somebody made a mistake in one number in my discharge book.

In the meantime I discussed my case with friends from the Air force: Aharon Remez, Dan Tolkovsky and Ezer Weizman and I am now sure I was discharged on 23.8.51, a few months after Remez, and afterwards I was probably on paid leave vacation.

I am not familiar with the laws and how you decide who is entitled to a pension but what I know is that I dedicated my best years to the security of the State until I was fired and not exactly demobilized.

Many years ago, whilst I was still in the R.A.F, I was approached by Eliahu Golomb, Levy Avrahami and Teddy Kollek [In Cairo] to do different jobs for the Haganah, the most important one being saving Yehuda Arazi.

Even after my discharge I was involved in many special missions, especially in Africa and some of my friends from that time know what I am talking about.

While doing these assignments I neglected my family and my business. For many years I could not return to England because of what I did for the State.

I never expected nor asked for any compensation and believed it was an honour for me to do it. Today I am old and sick and cannot provide for my family.

I suppose there are not many people in my situation and I think there should be a way to pay me in the same way as is done for many other retired officers, even though their service was not longer than mine, not more dangerous and they did not lose as much as I did .
Please reconsider my case.

Harry Gregori Tursz- Fredkens , Colonel (Retired)"

As a result of Harry's letter, Ariel Sharon was approached by Aharon Remez, the former Chief of the Israeli Air Force, with a request that a special exception be made for Harry. Sharon replied to Remez in February 1983 that a solution was being sought for Harry and other officers in a similar situation. As it happened Sharon resigned from the Ministry soon after as a result of the Kahan Commission of Enquiry into the 1982 Lebanese Affair. It was left to Yitzhak Rabin, the next Minister of Defence, to arrange a special pension for Harry and provide better security of tenure for him and his family. In effect, through the services of Oshnat Bar at the Ministry of Defence, who took over Harry's case, the Ministry purchased the flat in which the family lived and only asked a very nominal rent.

On the matter of the *"loan"*, Eli personally visited the Foreign Ministry. He warned one of their officials that their reluctance to act on Harry's behalf vis a vis the Congolese authorities was liable to lead to disclosures about Israel's part in Lumumba's demise, that could create a political crisis with Zaire.

Eli also thought of ways to raise Harry's spirits. He first organised a trip, in February 1981 to the Air Force Museum at Hatserim in the Negev. Harry was invited with his son Micky, then about 13 years old. Present were also, Eli Eyal, Alex Zieloni and the Museum's curator, Turner, who later became Mayor of Beer Sheva. After a tour of the base and lunch, Harry was presented with a sculpted wing in recognition of his deeds in the IAF. This really pleased him. The second surprise for Harry was when, a while later, Eli took him together with Lilian to the house of Shalom Levin in Tsahala. Harry had previously known Shalom under the code name "Asaf". He had been the head of the Haganah in Cairo and had convinced Harry to smuggle Yehuda Arazi out to Italy. Harry was overjoyed to find that this was a special occasion in his honour which reunited the members of the Haganah cell that had been instrumental in Arazi's escape from the clutches of the British CID. The other guests included Munia Mardor, famed for his arms procurement activities in Europe before the creation of the State. It was he who had secretly driven Arazi to the train station in Rehovot in May 1945, for his trip to Alexandria. There was also Levi Avrahami, one of the Cairo Cell, who later became Police Chief of Jerusalem and one of the girls from the flat in Algiers, where Arazi had been temporarily hidden. At a certain point in the evening, Harry received a phone call from Aharon Remez, his old commander in the IAF. He was too ill to be at the time to be present at the gathering. Altogether, Harry passed a wonderful evening reminiscing with his old friends over that spectacular exploit.

About this period, Harry was also busy briefing his lawyers in Israel and Belgium in the case he was preparing against the Hasson Brothers.

Unfortunately for Harry, in a judgement handed down in June 1981, the Brussels court accepted that the Kuyena receipt was genuine and that consequently his case for embezzlement against the Hassons failed. More painful for Harry, was that he was fined 100,000 Belgian francs for launching a vexatious legal action. Harry's lawyer in Brussels wrote to his lawyer in Israel suggesting that the only way to annul the fine was to appeal against the decision and to get a written statement from Kuyena as to what happened in March 1961. He also remarked that there were considerable unpaid legal fees that Harry had to settle and that in addition an advance payment would have to be made if he was considering an appeal. In a subsequent letter he stated that Harry's new instructions to trigger a criminal action against the Hasson Brothers was not feasible given that the action complained of, namely the introduction of a false receipt, did not take place on Belgian soil. Not to be thwarted in this pursuit, Harry then wrote to the Zairian Military Attaché in Brussels demanding that, within three weeks, the General Auditor declare the receipt as being false, failing which, he would accept the court's view of its authenticity. As a consequence, this would point to the culpability of the Zairian authorities in the affair. Unsurprisingly Harry failed to obtain an answer,

Harry then wrote to David Kimche, the Director General, pointing out that officials of the Ministry had conspired against him in the arbitration and that this had been recognised by the court. He suggested that the least the Foreign Ministry could do was to pressurise the Zaire authorities to issue an opinion on the receipt.

All these initiatives smack of Harry's increasing desperation and possibly recognition that the chances of winning his appeal and getting his money back were diminishing at every turn of this convoluted saga.

In July 1983, at Harry's request, Ben used one of his frequent visits to the Congo to find Isaie Kuyena. The goal was to obtain some proof of what happened to the 11.7 million Congolese Francs that the Hassons had, purportedly, handed to him. Ben first contacted the former foreign minister and later Ambassador to the United Nations Justin Bomboko. Theirs was a longstanding relationship going back to their time at University in Belgium in the 1950s. Ben had also been best man at his wedding and often stayed with him in the Congo after he retired from public life. Through Bomboko's good offices and other local contacts in the Congo, Ben managed eventually to track Kuyena down in his village. He was in hiding from the Mobutu regime and was not keen to expose himself. Nevertheless, he allowed himself to be spirited into the Belgian Consulate one night and made a statement, which was duly notarised. The following is a translation of an extract from that statement, dated 25 July 1983:

"I Kuyena kwa Muzita Fwawantondo confirm having received from Hasson Brothers the sum of 11,700,000 Congolese Francs. Furthermore I swear that I only acted under the express order of my superior, namely the former head of the Provincial Government [Vital Moanda] and not of my own free will.

In trying to transfer the money to Europe the former head of the Provincial [central Congo] Government met various financial restrictions imposed by the former Central Government. Consequently he decided to use the money to avoid the risk of loss. That is why the money was used for various provincial projects, such as maintenance work on the Malaga-Luozi road and particularly to pay the salaries of public sector employees.

In order to avoid the risk of confusion I would draw to your attention that it is not Kuyena as an individual who has acted in this way, but a former Government Minister who went to pick up the money as instructed by his former head of the Provincial Government.

Thank you for your understanding.

Kuyena"

With much greater difficulty, Ben also found Vital Moanda, Kuyena's immediate superior, who in March 1961 had ordered the diversion of the funds But his state of health was so bad that Ben held back from questioning him.

Both Kuyena and Bomboko tried to convince Ben that the $210,000 must have been paid back to Harry many years before, but they provided no evidence to this effect. From their knowledge of Harry, they could not believe that he would have allowed such a debt to remain unpaid for so long.

Thanks to Ben's efforts, Harry had, at last, written confirmation of what happened to the money, but this was unlikely to help his appeal against the lower court's decision in the Hasson case. Nevertheless, Harry felt that Kuyena's admission of false accounting could provide him with some leverage on the Mobutu Government. He therefore wrote once more to the Zairian Ambassador in Tel Aviv indicating that there was now clear proof of embezzlement by officials of the then Government. As Harry wished to avoid publicising this fact, which could only prove embarrassing for the present Government, he requested that the money owed to him, namely $210,000 plus interest of $732,000 be paid to him by 25 September, without the usual bureaucratic delays. The implicit threat was that if, in the Court of Appeal, he was to present Kuyena's testimony, this could only result in adverse publicity for the Zairian Government in the European as well as the American press. Inevitably, this new ploy by Harry failed. On 16 March 1984, the Brussels Court of Appeal dismissed Harry's appeal and upheld the judgement of the lower court. As the hearing was not held in public, no publicity ensued.

One can surmise that the family finances must have suffered considerably from the costs Harry incurred in his constant but vain attempts to seek justice in the Belgian courts.

Undaunted as ever, Harry then called upon the services of his second cousin, the Executive Vice President of the B'nai Brith International in Washington, Dr.Donald Thursz. The intention was to use the prestige of his office to convince the Zairian authorities that, given Harry's precarious state, they should settle the affair on humanitarian grounds.

Whilst congratulating the Prime Minister of Zaire on the re-establishment of diplomatic relations with Israel, Dr. Thursz remarked, in a letter dated 10 June 1985, that it would be difficult for his organisation to encourage the American Jewish community to invest in Zaire in the absence of a satisfactory resolution of Harry's claim.

However again, aside from receiving letters showing a sympathetic attitude, nothing was forthcoming. These continuous failures to prod the Zairian authorities into settling the debt may explain Harry's suggestion to his son, that he threaten to mine the Zaire River in order to force Mobutu into submission. Ben declined to go ahead with this madcap idea.

Harry then wrote to Chaim Herzog, the President of the State of Israel to ask him to use his influence with Mobutu, whom he knew well. The letter is reproduced here in full as it portrays Harry's personal view of his efforts on behalf of the State of Israel over the years:

"30th 5.86
Dear Mr. President,

I am writing this letter to you as a last desperate resort, as all my efforts to obtain justice having proved futile.

I submit that I have been let down and abandoned by the State of Israel, which I served assiduously for many years and for which I made sacrifices-not the least of which is my health. My record speaks for itself -to mention only the highlights:

In 1945, whilst still a flight lieutenant in the RAF, I rescued Yehuda Arazi. You may verify this with his daughter Ruthy and son-in-law Gabriel Bach.

As one of the founders of the Israeli Air Force, I flew not only combat missions but also special missions (some of them of a delicate nature, at the request of Ben Gurion) on one of which I was badly wounded. You may refer to Dan Tolkowfsky, my one-time assistant, Ezer Weitzman and Aharon Remez. The Israeli Air Force has seen fit to bestow honours upon me.

In 1960 I carried out a highly classified operation in Zaire at the request of our Foreign Office, during the ambassadorship of Ehud Avriel.

As a mechanical engineer, I was partly responsible for the design and construction of the reactor at Dimona.

In 1960, having spent some time previously in the Belgian Congo and later in Zaire, as the advisor to President Kasavubu, I was requested by him to make a loan of convenience to the Department of Defence, in the amount of two hundred and ten thousand US dollars ($210,000). I did so, to my regret. Since then I have waged a constant and wide-ranging battle, at considerable expense, to get re-payment but in vain.

Zaire officials in Kinshasa and Washington were approached by the Bnai Brith International concerning my claim, but with no result, although they did not contest it. Our foreign Office refuses to get involved for their own political considerations.

Mobutu and his close associates are fully conversant with my case.

Knowing of your close association with him, I appeal to you to intervene on my behalf, so that, at long last justice may be done.

A word from Mobutu in the appropriate quarter will result in the repayment of this long-overdue debt.

I married for a second time late in life [actually, a third time] *and have a family to provide for after I am gone, which cannot be long now at my age and state of health.*

Trusting to be favoured with you help.

Yours Sincerely,

P.S.I would be pleased to visit you in Jerusalem, if you wish"

Three months later, there was a response from the Director General of the President's Office requesting further details of the affair.

Subsequently in October 1986, in response to a letter of appeal from Dan Tolkovski, David Kimche, the Director General of the Foreign Ministry, refuted claims that the Ministry was responsible for the injustices suffered by Harry. Nevertheless, he promised that the newly designated Ambassador to Zaire would pursue Harry's claim. In fact, on 16 October he was brought to Netanya by Shalom Levin to meet Harry and review the correspondence. He subsequently stated that a decision whether the Foreign Office should do anything in this case would be taken prior to his departure in November. Quite clearly this demarche proved to be as unsuccessful as all the previous ones.

Harry didn't just rely on correspondence to advance his case, he also sought meetings at the offices of prominent politicians of the time. In view of his increasing infirmity he was chauffeured to these meetings by either Lilian or Annette's husband, Mordechai. Annette's son, Schmulik, remembers his father coming home from one of these meetings with the left-wing Member of the Knesset, Shulamit Aloni. He was disgusted at her attitude towards Harry's plight. After listening to Harry's tale, she literally asked Mordechai to take him out of her office. Lilian, in turn, remembers a visit to a young Foreign Ministry official, who could hardly disguise his lack of interest. To say that there was a lack of compassion towards Harry is the least of the charges that could be levied against the Israeli establishment.

When Lilian actively took over the correspondence in 1987 because Harry's eyesight was 40% impaired, a change of tack is apparent. Rather than Harry continuing to chase the Zairian Government, the suggestion now was that the Israeli Foreign Ministry should do so, after accepting moral responsibility and repaying the debt to Harry. Approaches in this vein were made in a series of letters by Lilian to Ezer Weizman when he became a Government Minister. She stated that the African Department of the Foreign Ministry was 100% in favour of this approach and that it only needed the consent of the Prime Minister [Yitshak Shamir] for it to be put into effect. On 31 August 1987 Harry himself wrote to Aharon Remez, asking him to obtain the support of Shimon Peres, Yitzhak Rabin, the Defence Minister and Nissan Limor of the President's Office in this endeavour.

When Ezer Weizman finally *"washed his hands"* of the case in February 1988, Harry asked Yitzhak Rabin to intercede with Yitzhak Shamir and arrange for the Foreign Office to accept liability for the debt, as he was pursuing their instructions when it was incurred.

The final letter in the bunch dated 4 July 1988 was addressed in English to Lilian by Nissan Limor, the Director General of the office of the President.

"Dear Mrs. Fredkens,

Further to your letter of June 29th 1988, I was pleased to hear that the Foreign Ministry is taking steps to help you solve your problem, and indeed I was advised that the two ministers are dealing with your case. I sincerely hope that they will help you reach a satisfactory solution.

Since the matter is now being handled by the proper authorities, and in the light of the fact that it is not customary for the President to intervene in Government affairs, nor to approach Foreign Governments in instances such as these, there would seem to be no place for intervention by our office.

We trust that the two ministers, being acquainted with your husband's deeds on behalf of the State, will indeed do their utmost to find a speedy answer to your problem.

With all good wishes to you and Col. Fredkens
Sincerely yours,
Nissan Limor. Director General"

It will not surprise the reader to learn that there appears to have been no follow up by the ministers concerned. The moneys were never repaid either by the Congolese or the Israeli Government.

Over the next sixteen months, Harry's health deteriorated to an extent where he was hardly mobile and not in control of his functions. In response, Oshnat Bar ensured that the Government provided other facilities to ease the increasing physical burden on his family. This included all the medical and other necessities required to sustain a wheelchair-bound man. They also provided for the services of a carer for six hours a day whilst Lilian was at work. Mina, who would arrive home first from school, would then take over the carer's duties. As one can imagine this was a very difficult and often unpleasant task for such a young girl. Micky at the time was in the army and could not therefore help to look after his father. It was only when it became physically and psychologically impossible to look after Harry at home, that Lilian agreed to residential care for him. But by then it was in the last weeks of his life. At his funeral on 19 November 1989 in Netanya, some of his old friends attended as well as Oshnat Bar, who had done so much to ease Lilian's burden in those last years. Telegrams of condolence were received from Yitzhak Rabin and Ezer Weizman. At the " *Shiva"* (bereavement gathering), some of Micky's friends from the army spoke to Lilian.

They expressed surprise that they had never heard about Harry's work for the State in his younger days. Indeed, to this day his history has remained unknown to the wider public.

Hopefully these past chapters will have rectified this omission.

Reunion of the Cairo Haganah Cell in 1981

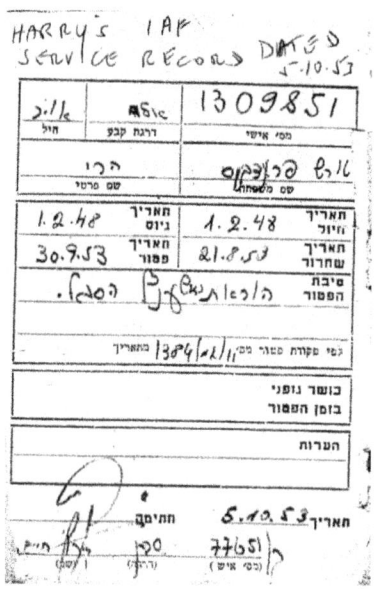

Harry's brief IAF record which confirms his 5 year
service from February 1948 to September 1953

```
                                    Cottage 11 San Martin
                                    Jerusalem, Israel
                                    September 27, 1982

Col. H. Fredkens Ret.
21 King David St.
Natanya 42264, Israel


Dear Freddy:
    In reply to your letter of September 20th, I hereby
confirm that at the time I relinquished command of the
I.A.F. you were still on active service in the Air
Force.
    I hope this will help you to establish your service
record and your ensuing rights.
    Wishing you a Happy New Year,
                                    Yours sincerely,

                                    Aharon Remez
```

Letter from Aharon Remez, head of the IAF from 1948 to 1953

Harry's friend, Dan Tolkowski.
These two photos span 53 years. The first reflects his role as head of the IAF from 1953 to 1958. The second photo was taken at his flat in Tel Aviv in 2006. He is now 98 years old.

To the left is Annette and next to Harry is his wife, Lilian on the patio of the flat in Netanya

Harry in Netanya at the time of his 80th birthday (1985)
With Annette are Harry's children, Micky, Mina and Ben

Harry and Lt./Col. (Reserves) Eli Eyal at Harry's 80th Birthday Party

Chapter 9: Family Views

[In some of the preceding chapters, I have recorded various incidents in Harry's Life, as recalled by members of his various families. In this chapter I set out the manner in which, in retrospect, he is perceived by those who were closest to him.]

Ben, his son from his first marriage:

Throughout the 70s and 80s Ben made several visits to Israel to see his father. He was always well received by both Harry's families. With his father though, he often despaired. Ben couldn't understand how Harry could be so clever at solving complex technical problems but was hopeless in other areas, such as conserving money. He would always put all his eggs in one basket. He wouldn't save. He always wanted to *"faire un coup"* (bring off a great financial deal). Harry always dreamed up hair-brained schemes involving millions of dollars. The possession of wealth was always very important to him, as he believed it gave you power over others. Yet status was not his goal. Even when he had low financial resources, he acted as if he was rich. He would always spend more money than he had. When he found himself short, Harry would borrow off friends, but he was not good at repaying his debts. At one time he was the only one in Leopoldville to have an expensive Jaguar car. He also bought and sold aeroplanes. It was never clear what was the source of his means. Harry was always very clever, very daring and not scared of anything. He always liked things to be dynamic. He couldn't rest. Although he was big, physically-speaking, it was his brain which dominated. So, he could take excellent short-term decisions but soon got bored with the project in hand and so nothing ever worked for any length of time, as was evidenced by his business failures in Israel. His business partners always seemed to get out at the right time and Harry was left with unsaleable merchandise or a property deal which went sour. Another of Harry's failings was his taste for unwise litigation. Particularly when he was broke, he always felt that others were out to do him out of his money. As we have seen, both the Hasson Brothers and the Republic of the Congo fell within this category.

Ben became particularly perturbed when Harry in the early1960s interested himself in dubious arms deals involving Israeli and Swedish manufacturers and customers who would bid the most. He was forever studying arms catalogues. Ben, who disliked this trade, believed that, despite the risks that Harry was taking, it was never very profitable for him.

Ben was very sceptical about Harry's support for Zionism. He believed that his actions were dictated more by his sense of adventure than by any real sense of commitment. Harry tremendously enjoyed making war in all its forms, covert and overt and maybe here, according to Ben, lay the key to all his heroic acts.

Ben, despite Harry's obvious deterioration and bitterness in his last years, will always want to retain the best possible image of his father. This to some extent explains Ben's reluctance to reveal some details of his father's life which Harry himself would have preferred to keep secret. This position Ben studiously maintained during my two extensive interviews with him in Brussels

Once with in wry smile, Ben said:

"What in his life was fact and what is legend is often difficult for me to say Some aspects are very brilliant, some like his (real or imaginary role) in the Lumumba Affair are probably best forgotten"

Ben confirmed Harry's known streak of stubbornness, authoritarianism and hubris. One thing Ben was very clear about, however, and that was his admiration for Lilian, Harry's third wife. He regarded her as an angel for the way she attended to Harry during his last years.[21]

Lilian, his third wife;

She always accepted Harry as she found him. He gave her the children that she wanted and, in the early years at least, a comfortable existence in Israel. She coped with his changing moods, initially caused by business failures and later his obsessive preoccupation with the Congolese debt. When times turned bad in 1972, she stuck by him, uncomplaining and loyal as always. She recognised that intellectually she could never be his equal but that did not give her a complex. Unlike Harry she could stick to a job and accepted with good grace having to return to work to maintain her family. Throughout Harry's deteriorating health in the 1980s she tended to him and only in the last weeks of his life recognised that she could no longer give him the 24-hour nursing care that he required. She devoted 25 years of her life to him and did not regret one moment of it, despite the many difficulties she had to endure.

Mina, his daughter from his third marriage:

Mina remembers her father as being always immaculately dressed like an English gentleman. He would never go out, like other Israelis wearing shorts or other very casual clothes. He was generous to a fault, as Mina said: *"If you wanted the moon, he would bring it to you"*. He never spoke about the past but was constantly working on his typewriter and the children understood that he needed his space. As he grew older and was affected by illness, he

---

[21] Ben died in Brussels in July 2019 at the age of 85.

became more irascible and difficult. Although he was her father, he couldn't always give her what she needed from him and her mother's absence at work compounded her feeling of loneliness. It was a difficult childhood only alleviated by her friends. She was aware that money was a constant problem and that Harry sought to preserve whatever he had. From the time when Mina was 14, (1986) Harry was in serious decline. He couldn't bear that, in the absence of Lilian at work or his carer, Mina had to deal with his more personal needs, and he would try to push her away.

During our discussion about Harry she was at least twice overcome by emotion and I had to curtail my questioning.

Micky, his son from his third marriage:

Micky was initially restrained when talking about his father but opened up gradually. As he was 5 years older than Mina he remembered vaguely the early days with his parents in Caesarea, before they had to move. As there were few families around there were also few children, but this improved when they arrived in Pardes Hannah and he went to the kinder garden. After the quality of their living accommodation in Caesarea and Pardes Hannah, the apartment they were able to afford in Netanya came as something of a let-down. Micky remembers that when the Yom Kippur war started in October 1973 and the sirens went, Harry refused to go down to the basement shelter. In the following years there were two more moves within Netanya until they ended up in a penthouse. Much of that time Harry was constantly abroad on business trying to earn a living, whilst Lilian was rearing the children. It was only later when the children went to school that she took up the job at the Diamond Centre. Micky never felt that he and his sister were deprived of anything because of the family's poor finances. Basically, they lived the life of a lower middle-class family in Israel at that time.

When Harry died in 1989, Micky had just finished his 3 years in the army. Although Micky had briefly heard of Harry's exploits, he never really explored these with him in any depth possibly because, by the time Micky showed any interest, his father was too old to relate the details. However, the subject of the Congolese loan was, in the 1980s, a constant refrain in their household as was Harry's sense of having been badly let down by the establishment.

In Micky's view, the physical difficulties which Harry suffered in his last years, did not distress him half as much as the degeneration of his mental faculties.

These, as we have gathered through these pages, had been so essential to the strength of his intellect that to be unable to concentrate for any length of time or to recall details must have been the ultimate frustration for a man of his calibre.

Annette, Harry's one-time stepdaughter:

To all intents and purposes, Annette regarded Harry as her father from the time she first met him in 1945. She was then 6 years old and was enthralled when Harry took her and her mother to the Congo for the first time at the end of 1946. Annette, in contrast to Ben, maintains that he looked after his workers at the mill, and did not treat them as a Belgian colonial master. Nevertheless, in her twenties, she had few remaining illusions about Harry's flaws and, after her own marriage to Mordechai in 1962, was not surprised by her mother's desire for a divorce from him. She recounted that Harry had had an affair with a saleslady at her aunt's shop, which Ida was aware of but, in this instance, let it pass. In Annette's view, Ida's ultimate desire for a divorce was more related to Harry's long absences in Europe, and the feelings of financial insecurity, than Harry's occasional peccadilloes. Annette's own period of estrangement from Harry was short-lived and she and her family continued to see him until he died. Her contacts with Lilian remain warm. Harry had the great facility of bringing all the strands of his three marriages together so that his children all knew and appreciated each other. He even managed to introduce Ida and much later Lilian to Rosette. But unaccountably he never introduced Lilian to Ida. Harry was one of a kind, a complex and flawed man but to Annette, a substitute father she will always remember with great affection.

Schmulik, Annette's son:

Schmulik recalled that for a time, in the early 1970s, Annette and Harry were estranged. He had inveigled her in a financial dealing involving post-dated cheques which Harry had provided as security for money he borrowed from her. Unfortunately, the cheques bounced. But then, after a year or two Mordechai met him in the street and was surprised how much he had deteriorated in the intervening period. This broke the ice for a reconciliation to be effected and henceforth on a Saturday, Annette and her family would visit Netanya. For Mordechai this was a hardship because he couldn't stand all the animals that also occupied the flat, and the smell that went with it. For Schmulik and his sister, Miri, Harry was known as Grandpa Harry, despite the lack of any biological connection.

Chapter 10 Conclusion

I did not know, until I had re-read my manuscript many times, what sort of final assessment of Harry's life I would come to. In the end I do not believe that the gaps in the information available, which I have often referred to, would have made much of a difference to the overall view of the man I have portrayed.

It is of course for each reader to assess Harry in the light of his or her own sense of values and life experiences. But the context of the times in which Harry lived and the challenges he faced in each of his varied roles, are important matters to consider, in making a personal judgement.

For myself, I cannot deny that I am captivated by this truly remarkable man. He lived his life according to his own zeitgeist and constantly adjusted to the situations which presented themselves to him. I admire the way he always tried to work his way through the many perils and pitfalls he encountered, many of them self-inflicted. It would have been wonderful to have met him and I am envious of those members of my family who did.

I have been particularly struck by the consistency of the love and affection he engendered despite the hurt and pain he occasionally caused to his various families during his extraordinary lifetime. Again, the selfless endeavours, in later life, of his former IAF and Haganah companions, to remedy his financial decline are testimony of their enduring respect for his accomplishments in the service of the State.

His courage was second to none and he fought ferociously against injustices, he truly believed, others made him endure. His ongoing correspondence with Israeli personalities to the end of his days is witness to his incredible fortitude. Always, his underlying concern was to provide a financial safeguard for his wife and children. He himself knew that the progressive deterioration in his health could only have one result and yet he never truly gave up.

May he rest in peace.

Appendix: 1

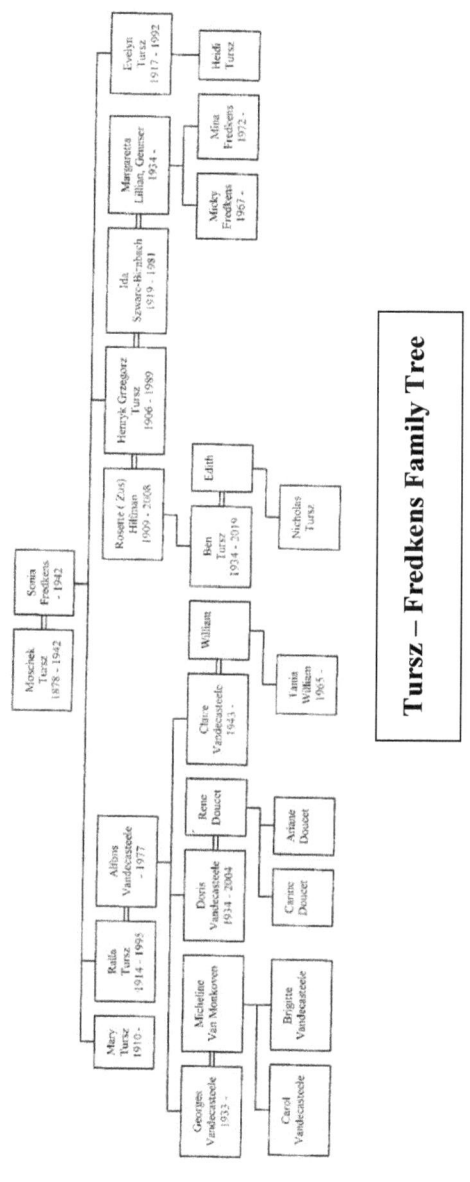

Lightning Source UK Ltd.
Milton Keynes UK
UKHW011814151219
355432UK00001B/173/P